DØ968874

The Collections of the Royal Geographical Society (with IBG) were used to research some of the details in this book. It is stimulating to see them used in such an inspirational way. The book should encourage children of all ages to find out more about the world they live in and how it is formed.

GEOGRAPHY HAS NEVER BEEN SUCH FUN BEFORE!

**Judith Mansell – Education Officer,
Royal Geographical Society**

Horrible Geography

INTREPID EXPLORERS

ANITA GANERI

Illustrated by
Mike Phillips

Hippo

To Jacob. With love A.G.

Also available:

Violent Volcanoes
Odious Oceans
Stormy Weather
Raging Rivers
Desperate Deserts
Earth-shattering Earthquakes
Freaky Peaks
Bloomin' Rainforests
Perishing Poles

Scholastic Children's Books,
Euston House, 24 Eversholt Street,
London NW1 1DB, UK
a division of Scholastic Ltd
London ~ New York ~ Toronto ~ Sydney ~ Auckland
Mexico City ~ New Delhi ~ Hong Kong

First published in the UK by Scholastic Ltd, 2003

Text copyright © Anita Ganeri, 2003
Illustrations copyright © Mike Phillips, 2003

10 digit ISBN 0 439 98137 9
13 digit ISBN 978 0439 98137 8

All rights reserved

Typeset by M Rules
Printed and bound by Nørhaven Paperback A/S, Denmark

6 8 10 9 7

The right of Anita Ganeri and Mike Phillips to be identified as the author and illustrator of this
work respectively has been asserted by them in accordance with the Copyright, Designs and
Patents Act, 1988.

CONTENTS

INTRØDUCTIØN

Geography can be a pain in the neck. Especially if you nod off in your geography lesson and your head's at an awkward angle. Picture the scene. One minute, you're sitting at your desk, listening to your teacher's voice droning drearily on...

TODAY'S LESSON IS ALL ABOUT FLOCCULATION.* HANDS UP IF YOU KNOW WHAT I'M TALKING ABOUT?

*Roughly translated, flocculation is the tricky technical term for the way soil forms into clumps. Just the sort of earth-shatteringly boring fact geography teachers love.

The next thing you know, you're happily snoozing away, and you're having a fantastic dream. Get this. You're a world-famous explorer just back from your latest trail-blazing trip. You've climbed a brand-new freaky peak, unknown to geography, and the reporters are going wild.

I NAME THIS FREAKY PEAK AFTER... ME!

GOOD CHOICE!

The world is your oyster. Anything is now possible. Fame and fortune beckon... But before all this attention goes to your head, you wake up with a nasty start. Your teacher's shrill words bring you back down to Earth with a bump (and a horrible crick in your neck).

People have been exploring for centuries, risking their lives in far-flung places that no one's ever set foot in before. Some have gone mad, turned bad or dropped dead from a dreadful disease. Many others have ended up lost. Hopelessly lost. So why on Earth did they do it? The truth is that lots of them were in it for the money. They wanted to open up the world for trade and make lots of lovely lolly. Others wanted to claim new lands to live in, or spread their religious ideas. But many were horrible geographers and scientists. They simply wanted to see the world and fill in the gaps on the maps.

Of course, it takes real guts to be an explorer, but if you're not brave enough to be one just yet, don't despair. The good news about Horrible Geography is that you can follow in the footsteps of famous explorers without having to leave home. So why not settle back in a comfy sofa, grab yourself a snack and a tin of pop, and get ready to head off on the trip of a lifetime. In *Intrepid Explorers*, you will...

- dice with death as you sail the world's stormiest seas.

- brave blinding blizzards to reach the perishing Poles.

- risk your life on a raging river on a wild-goose chase for gold.

- meet the not-so-intrepid explorer who *didn't* actually like travelling.

This is geography like never before. And it's horribly exciting. But be warned. Some of the travellers' tales in this book contain spine-chilling details of disease, disaster and death. And they're all true – unfortunately. Luckily, you'll have budding explorer Miles to keep you company on your travels. Still keen to be off? Well, good luck and have a good trip!

INTREPID
ANCIENT
EXPLØRERS

A very long time ago, about 3.5 million years before your geography teacher was born, our ape-like ancestors came down from the trees and began to walk upright. You could say they learned to stand on their own two feet. Ha ha! Meet the first intrepid explorers…

Early humans were as curious about the big, wide world as little kids in a sweet shop. But they also needed to keep moving to survive. They travelled long distances to hunt for food, find shelter and steer clear of the gruesome glaciers that covered the Earth. Of course, they didn't realize they were actually exploring. After all, they had no idea where on Earth they were going. No one had seen these places before. And there weren't any handy maps to help them. They just had to follow their noses.

But oddly, the real story of exploration began thousands of years ago when people started to settle down. Perhaps all that staying in one place gave them itchy feet? They set off to find new lands to live in and new goods to trade.

Luckily for horrible geographers, some of them left records of their journeys so we know roughly where they went. Fancy a quick trip to Ancient Egypt?

The intrepid Egyptians

In around 3500 BC, the awesome Ancient Egyptians built the first sailing boats. They were made from papyrus (smashed-up reeds) and had square sails for when it was windy (and oars for when it was not). These boats were brilliant for sailing trips on the River Nile. Later the Egyptians built ships out of tougher timber for exploring the big, wide world.

Destination: Punt

There was one place in particular which the Egyptians loved to visit. It was called Punt and legend said it was the Land of the Gods. The streets of Punt weren't just paved with gold. Oh no. Punt was crammed full of precious ebony (a type of dark wood), ivory, baboons, leopards, myrrh and frankincense (that's smelly stuff burned in Egyptian temples). No wonder intrepid Egyptian explorers couldn't wait to get there, even though the round trip took over a year through shark-infested waters.

In 1492 BC, the ruler of Egypt, Queen Hatshepsut, had a brilliant idea. She was having a posh new tomb built for herself and it needed decorating. And what better to use than the riches of Punt? Of course, the Queen couldn't go herself. She was far too busy ruling Egypt. Instead she sent a fleet of five ships and 250 sailors to search for the legendary land. But pinpointing Punt wasn't all plain sailing. You see, since the last voyage there, 500 years before, its precise location had been forgotten and it was two gruelling years before they finally found it again. Luckily the sailors brought back boatloads of priceless treasure, and the Queen was as pleased as Punt, sorry, punch. So pleased, in fact, that she had the walls of her tomb decorated with scenes from the epic voyage.

The globe-trotting Greeks

The Ancient Greeks were real clever-clogs. They were always dreaming up brilliant new theories to explain how the world went round. For instance:

- They guessed the Earth spun on its axis and moved round the sun. (But it wasn't until the seventeenth century that anyone believed them.)

- They worked out that the Earth was round when everyone else thought it was flat. (Yep. People really believed if you went too far one way, you'd plummet off the edge.)

- They calculated the size of the Earth within a few hundred kilometres or so. (Long before anyone else did.)

Pretty impressive, eh? Of course, the Ancient Greeks also had some very strange ideas about geography. For example, they sailed happily around the Mediterranean Sea, fighting wars and exploring foreign countries. And they knew that the great Western Sea (that's the Atlantic Ocean to you and me) lay beyond the Med. But would they sail into the Western Sea itself? No way. They were too bloomin' scared. It was too wild and stormy, they said, and full of terrible sea monsters who liked eating sailors for lunch. So there.

Earth-shattering fact

The way into the Western Sea lay through a narrow channel of water, wedged between two towering pillars of rock. But it hadn't always been like this. According to legend, the great Greek hero Heracles had to perform a series of superhuman tasks set for him by the gods.

Setting off on one of his amazing adventures, he found his way out of the Med blocked by gigantic rocks. This didn't stop Heracles. He simply ripped the rocks up with his bare hands and forced a passage through. Then he plonked the rocks down on either side to guard the Med. The Greeks called them the Pillars of Heracles after our hero. (We now call the passage the Straits of Gibraltar.)

It needed a horribly hardy explorer to follow in Heracles's footsteps. Someone who wasn't scared stiff of sailing between the perilous Pillars and out into the unknown. Luckily, the Ancient Greeks had just the man for the job. Are you ready to meet him?

Horrible Geography Travellers' Tales

Pytheas was born in Marseilles, France. (Though in those days Marseilles was called Massalia and was part of Ancient Greece.) Marseilles was a bustling port and perhaps it was seeing all those ships that gave Pytheas a taste for travel. No one knows much about Pytheas's life or his family, or exactly when he lived. But we do know he was a genius at geography and astronomy so he must have gone to school.

In around 330 BC, Pytheas made an astonishing voyage to the very edge of the known world. At least, that was his story and he was sticking to it. Here's a map of the route (he said) he took:

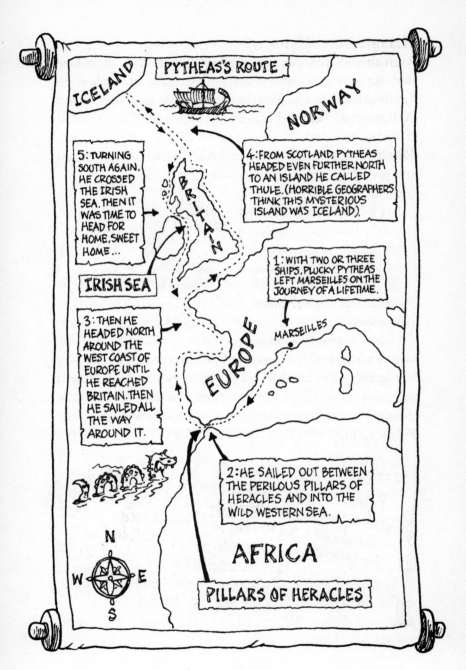

PYTHEAS'S ROUTE

ICELAND

NORWAY

5: TURNING SOUTH AGAIN, HE CROSSED THE IRISH SEA. THEN IT WAS TIME TO HEAD FOR HOME, SWEET HOME...

4: FROM SCOTLAND, PYTHEAS HEADED EVEN FURTHER NORTH TO AN ISLAND HE CALLED THULE. (HORRIBLE GEOGRAPHERS THINK THIS MYSTERIOUS ISLAND WAS ICELAND).

BRITAIN

1: WITH TWO OR THREE SHIPS, PLUCKY PYTHEAS LEFT MARSEILLES ON THE JOURNEY OF A LIFETIME.

IRISH SEA

3: THEN HE HEADED NORTH AROUND THE WEST COAST OF EUROPE UNTIL HE REACHED BRITAIN. THEN HE SAILED ALL THE WAY AROUND IT.

MARSEILLES

EUROPE

2: HE SAILED OUT BETWEEN THE PERILOUS PILLARS OF HERACLES AND INTO THE WILD WESTERN SEA.

N

W E

S

AFRICA

PILLARS OF HERACLES

18

Tall tales or true stories?

Even though Pytheas was the first Greek ever to explore that far north, no hero's welcome greeted him when he finally arrived home. And no fame or fortune either. Why? Well, nobody believed a word Pytheas said. They scoffed at his stories and accused him of telling a pack of lies. Here's what one of his critics said (when he'd stopped sniggering):

Any man who has told such great falsehoods about the known regions would hardly, I imagine, be able to tell the truth about places that are not known to anybody.

How on Earth could poor Pytheas convince them he was telling the truth? He decided to write down everything he'd seen and called his book *Description of the Ocean*. But that didn't do the trick. Sadly, no copies exist today, but Polybius, another Greek, read it and this is what he thought:

Pytheas says that the seas around Thule are covered in wobbly jellyfish. Very fishy. He should have had his eyes tested before he left Greece. He also says that, in the far north, the Sun shines all night in summer but doesn't rise in winter at all. Now that really is going too far.

Clearly Polybius thought Pytheas was a frightful fibber and didn't believe a word he had written. But incredibly it turned out that Pytheas had been telling the truth all along.

Horrible geographers now know Pytheas was right. Although he probably didn't see any actual jellyfish, in winter the sea around Iceland (Thule) is covered in clear, round, blobs of pancake ice that could look like jellyfish from a distance. As for the sun, he was right again. Pytheas was describing the midnight sun. In the far north, in summer it's daylight all the time and in winter it's permanently dark. What happens is this. During the year, the Earth orbits (circles round) the sun. It also tilts over at an angle on its axis. This means that the far north is tilted away from the sun in winter and towards it in summer. Got all that?

Of course, all of this was discovered far too late for poor Pytheas. He spent the rest of his life trying desperately to prove he was right. Fortunately, the intrepid explorers in the next section didn't have that particular problem. No, instead they had a rather rocky road to pass…

Meandering monks

Thousands of years ago, Europe and Asia were linked by ancient roads. Merchants travelled vast distances along them to buy and sell luxury goods. The most famous road of all was called the old Silk Road, though it was actually made up of several different routes across Asia and the Middle East into Europe. It was the way that precious silk from China reached Europe.

Teacher teaser

Is your teacher an old smoothie? Or is she always losing the thread? Put up your hand, smile your silkiest smile and ask her this harmless-sounding question:

PLEASE, MISS, WHERE DOES SILK COME FROM?

a) It grows on silk trees.
b) It's spun by silk moth bugs.
c) It's made in a silk factory.

21

Answer: b) Silk is made from silk moth cocoons. They're cases which silk moth bugs hide in when they change from caterpillars into adult moths. Long ago, silk was all the rage. Rich ancient Romans couldn't get enough of the shiny stuff which was brought along the old Silk Road from China. But they hadn't a clue how silk was actually made. For thousands of years, the crafty Chinese kept silk-making top secret. After all, silk was big business and they didn't want anyone else nabbing a share. And the Silk Road wasn't just useful for shifting silk. It was also a brilliant way for intrepid explorers to see more of the world. Bet your teacher didn't know all that!

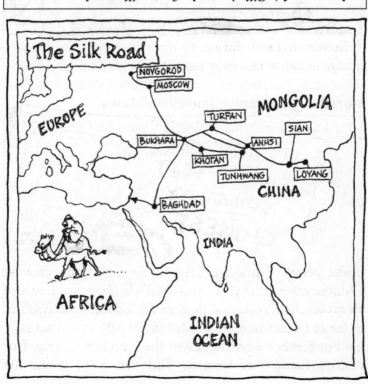

22

A long and winding road

The old Silk Road wasn't a nice paved road like the ones you get today. This rocky route led through monstrous mountains, bone-dry deserts and plummeting river ravines. Worse still, it was guarded by bloodthirsty bandits who thought nothing of murdering merchants and other unwary travellers, and stealing their money and goods.

So why on Earth did a mild-mannered monk from China decide to follow this risky road? You're about to find out…

Horrible Geography Travellers' Tales

Some people think that Hsuan Tsang was the greatest Chinese explorer ever. He was also a brilliant student and all his teachers reckoned he'd go far. Though perhaps not as far as India where he headed in AD 629. It was actually his big brother who suggested the treacherous trip. But Hsuan Tsang was keen to find out more about his

Buddhist faith. (Buddhism began in India in the sixth century BC.) He wanted to bring some holy books home to translate from Sanskrit (an ancient Indian language) into Chinese. Little did he think it would be 15 long years before he saw his home again…

Earth-shattering fact
Hsuan Tsang was following in the footsteps of another meandering monk called Fa Hsien (AD 370–?). He set off for India in AD 399. When he got back to China he wrote a thrilling book about his travels. He didn't want to write it at first. He was worried about setting a bad example. He said:

If I were to tell what has happened to me, then people of unstable mind might be tempted to take the same risks, reckless of their personal safety. For they would argue that I came back safe and sound. So these foolish persons would set about jeopardizing their lives in lands impossible to explore, and which only one in ten thousand men could hope to come out of alive.

But even these wise words of warning didn't stop hardy Hsuan Tsang.

Almost at once, disaster struck. First, Hsuan Tsang had to sneak out of China because he didn't have the Emperor's permission to leave. (In those days, you needed the Emperor's say-so to do just about anything.) Then he headed west along the old Silk Road. Unfortunately, the guide he'd hired to lead him across the gruesome Gobi Desert, er, deserted him. There was nothing but sand for miles and miles, and Hsuan Tsang soon got hopelessly lost.

All he could do was plod on, alone except for his trusty old horse. Then things went from bad to worse. Hsuan Tsang lost his water bag and nearly died of thirst. (Bet he wished his brother had kept his big mouth shut.) But just as he hit rock bottom, Hsuan Tsang had a stroke of luck. A local king took pity on him and sent the miserable monk on with another guide and a load of goodies for the journey.

Eventually, Hsuan Tsang reached India where he spent the next 13 years. Like Fa Hsien before him, he visited masses of Buddhist monasteries and holy sites, learned Sanskrit and Buddhist philosophy (I told you he was brainy), and collected loads of precious manuscripts to take back to China. Some time in AD 643, Hsuan Tsang headed north to start the long journey home. But if he thought it would be a doddle compared to his journey there, he was wrong. Horribly wrong. If he'd kept a secret diary, it might have looked something like this:

My secret diary
by Hsuan Tsang
(Not to be read by the Emperor)

Some time in AD 643
What a disaster! I reached the River Indus safely – so far, so good. But a storm blew up and almost capsized our little boat. And 50 of my best manuscripts and all the rare seeds I'd collected fell into the wretched river, never to be seen again.

What's more, I've been given a pesky elephant to ride across the mountains. Apparently it's a great honour, but I'm not so sure. It's an ugly-looking brute with a nasty glint in its eyes. And it never stops eating. I only wish it had drowned instead of my lovely books.

Later in AD 643
I didn't mean it, sob, about the elephant. If only I could take it back. Guess what? It's only gone and drowned. And it's all my fault. A few days ago, we were attacked by bandits. What a bunch! Not content with pinching our money, they wanted to throw me into the river as a sacrifice to the gods. I thought I was a goner, I really did. But then I heard an enormous splash right behind me. The elephant was so freaked out it panicked and jumped in the river. Oh dear, where's my hanky?

Homeward bound
Intrepid Hsuan Tsang finally reached China in AD 645. He'd travelled over 12,000 kilometres – a staggering feet, sorry, feat, for the time. He brought back copies of hundreds of holy books (he had the lost ones copied again)

and other souvenirs of his trip. In fact, he had so much luggage it took 20 horses to carry it all. The Emperor gave Hsuan Tsang a hero's welcome (he'd forgiven him for giving him the slip) and ordered him to write an official account of his amazing travels. As if Hsuan Tsang hadn't got enough to do, translating all those books.

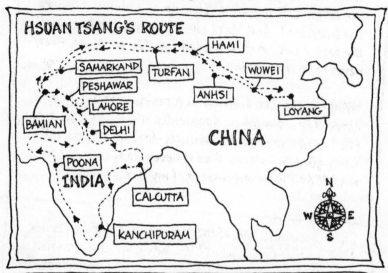

HSUAN TSANG'S ROUTE

HAMI · SAMARKAND · TURFAN · WUWEI · PESHAWAR · ANHSI · LAHORE · LOYANG · BAMIAN · DELHI · CHINA · POONA · INDIA · CALCUTTA · KANCHIPURAM

Our next brave adventurer didn't set out to become an intrepid explorer. It was all the idea of his dear old dad. But, like hardy Hsuan Tsang, he got to know the old Silk Road very well indeed.

Plucky Marco Polo

In 1271, young Marco Polo set out on the journey of a lifetime. Instead of having to go to school, lucky Marco got to go to far-flung China and back. How cool is that?

Horrible Geography Travellers' Tales

Marco's dad was a wealthy merchant and when Marco was a lad, he left him with his mother and sailed off to Constantinople (now Istanbul) in Turkey. Marco didn't see him again for nine years. Think of all that pocket money he must have missed. In those days, Marco's home town of Venice was a rich and busy port. Marco must have watched the ships come and go, hoping for a postcard from his distant dad…

Constantinople, Turkey, 1261

Dear Son,

The journey was fine and I got here safely. Sorry you couldn't come. Business is booming. I've already sold a load of jewels and made loads of lovely dosh. Tomorrow I'm off to China so I'll write again when I get there. Now you be a good boy for your mother. And don't forget to go to school. See you soon. Love from Dad..xxx

P.S. I'll give you your pocket money when I get back.

When Marco was about 16 years old, his mum died and his dad came home. But he didn't stay for long. Soon he was off on his travels again, only this time he took young Marco along for the ride.

A dreadful journey

In China, Marco's dad had made friends with the great ruler Kublai Khan. The Khan told him to come back soon and bring him some presents. But not any old pressies, like pairs of socks or bubble bath that your dear old granny gives you for Christmas. No, the crafty Khan wanted 100 priests to do magic tricks and some oil from a holy lamp burning in Jerusalem.

Luckily, the Polos had friends in high places. In 1271 they travelled to Jerusalem to pick up the oil, and the Pope sent them some priests. OK, there were only two priests, not the 100 the Khan had wanted, and even they soon  scarpered. But now the journey to China could begin in earnest. The Polos' plan was to follow the Silk Road for most of its length through Central Asia and into the Far East. No one had ever done this before. It was far too risky.

The journey was appalling. First, Marco fell ill and had to stay in bed for a year. Then, as soon as he'd recovered, they climbed the perilous Pamir Mountains. But worse was to come. It was too risky to travel alone, so they hitched a lift with a passing caravan to cross the desperate

Gobi Desert. No, not the sort of caravan you go on holiday in today. This caravan was made up of hundreds of camels or donkeys and carried goods like silk. The desert was said to be haunted and at night they heard ghostly voices and noises like beating drums. Spooky, or what?

A horrible geographer would say "Haunted? Pah! What a load of codswallop. The sounds they heard were made by desert rocks shrinking in the cold night air after they'd expanded in the baking daytime heat. Then again... Aagghhhh, what's that noise? I'm outta here!"

WHOOOOO,,,

China, at last

Finally, in 1275, the plucky Polos reached China. They were given a warm welcome by Kublai Khan (though he was a bit miffed about the missing priests). Their journey had taken three and a half years, and they'd covered some 6,000 kilometres. Did Marco mind? Not a bit. He thought China was brilliant and he didn't have time to be homesick. He stayed in Kublai Khan's posh palace and learned to speak the local language. Kublai Khan liked Marco so much he gave him the job of exploring his empire and bringing back news of what he'd seen. It was the perfect job for Marco. For the next 17 years, while his dad was busy with his business, Marco travelled thousands of kilometres and saw many strange and wonderful things. His favourite place was the fabulous city of Kinsai, in the east of China. Its name meant "The City of Heaven". Marco described it as a rich and busy place, criss-crossed with bridges and canals. Besides, it was perfect for parties, which were held on two islands in the middle of the lake. How heavenly is that?

Voyage to Venice
All good things come to an end, and in 1292 the Polos headed for home. This time they chose a short-cut, sailing around India instead of going overland. They set off in January in a Chinese junk (that's junk as in ship, not a load of rubbish) as part of a fleet of 14 ships and 600 courtiers. You see, a local princess was going to Persia to get married and the Khan asked the Polos to escort her. But the voyage went from bad to worse. Some of the ships were wrecked on rocks and lots of passengers drowned or died from deadly diseases. The Polos were lucky to escape with their lives. But at least the princess reached Persia safely. When the Polos finally reached Venice in 1295, most of their

friends and relations had given them up for dead. So you can imagine what a stir their arrival caused – especially when they cut open the seams of their strange Chinese clothes to reveal a small fortune in jewels stuffed inside.

Marco's memoirs

But our Marco wasn't the sort of person to settle down and put his feet up. In 1298 he went off to fight the Genoese* but was captured and thrown in prison. As luck would have it, he shared his cramped prison cell with a writer called Rustichello. To pass the days, Marco told Rustichello his incredible life story and Rustichello wrote it down in a book.

*People from Genoa. The cities of Venice and Genoa went to war over who controlled the best trade routes.

The book was called *The Book of Ser Marco Polo the Venetian Concerning the Kingdoms and Marvels of the East*. What a mouthful. Even so, it quickly became a best-seller. Readers couldn't get enough of Marco's amazing adventures. There was just one teeny hitch. Some of his adventures were so amazing that people thought Marco must have made them up. It didn't help that Rustichello was used to writing novels about love and all that slushy stuff. He thought a book full of facts would be boring so he exaggerated things a bit. For example, instead of writing...

Today we climbed a snow-capped mountain. It was hard to breathe and I got a blister.

…he might have written something mushy like…

THIS FINE MORN WE TRAVERSED A WONDEROUS PEAK, WITH ITS DELICATE DUSTING OF ELFIN WHITE. MY HEART SANG WITH WONDERMENT AND MY FEET DANCED WITH DELIGHT…

See what I mean?

Marco's super sightseeing quiz

So had all this sightseeing gone to Marco's head? Or was he telling the truth all along? Here are five strange sights he said he'd seen on his travels. Try this quick quiz to find out if they're far-fetched falsehoods or terrific truths.

1 Black stones that burned like wood.
TRUE/FALSE?

2 People with long, thick tails and dogs' heads.
TRUE/FALSE?

3 A white cloth that couldn't catch fire.
TRUE/FALSE?

4 A nut as big as your head and covered in hair.
TRUE/FALSE?

5 A giant bird as big as an elephant.
TRUE/FALSE?

Answers:

1 TRUE. The burning stones were coal which was used as fuel to heat bathwater. In China, Marco noted, people actually enjoyed having baths. Yes, I know it's hard to believe!

2 FALSE. This was the sort of tall tale early European explorers loved making up. For good measure, there's also a picture in Marco's book of a one-legged giant which used its massive foot as a giant sunshade. Unbelievable.

3 TRUE. The white cloth was asbestos. It's found in rocks and is crushed up to form fibres for making cloth and ropes. It was once used in buildings to stop fires spreading but it's horribly dangerous if you breathe in its dust.

4 TRUE. This tough nut was a coconut which Marco saw in south-east Asia. His report said the flesh was delicious to eat and the milk tasted like wine.

5 TRUE. Well, almost. What Marco probably saw was an enormous elephant bird. It lived on the island

of Madagascar and stood three metres tall. Marco said it swooped down like an eagle and picked up elephants to eat. Actually, you'll be pleased to know, elephant birds couldn't fly. But you'll have to take my word for it. These monster birds became extinct about 300 years ago.

Only half the story

You can't really blame Marco's readers if they couldn't believe their eyes. They'd never read anything like it before. Most of them had never left Italy and hadn't a clue about the outside world. But the bickering didn't stop. Even when Marco was on his deathbed, someone asked him to admit he'd been fibbing. Marco replied he'd only revealed half of what he'd seen. If he'd told the rest, he added, nobody would have believed a word! Luckily all that was to change. Marco's intrepid travels had opened up a whole new world for Europeans and soon other dead famous explorers were following in his footsteps. All aboard for some adventures on the high seas…

SUFFERING SAILORS

For centuries, seafaring explorers have set sail in search of fame, fortune and adventure. Many of them were merchants who went to look for short-cuts to far-flung places to trade. Others went to find new lands to live in and claim for their own countries. But it wasn't all plain sailing. If you thought life on the ocean wave was one long holiday, think again. Our intrepid sailors suffered horribly…

For a start, the odious oceans are ENORMOUS. They cover about two-thirds of the planet, which is an awful lot of seawater to get lost in. Suffering sailors didn't have many maps and charts to guide them, and the ones they had were often woefully wrong. Instead sailors had to rely on the sun and stars to find their way from A to B. What if it was a cloudy day? Well, then they got hopelessly lost!

Earth-shattering fact
The plucky Phoenicians were superb sailors who explored the Mediterranean over 2,000 years ago. Mostly they were in it for money, trading in timber, tin and a precious dye made from a kind of shellfish. Bet you were dyeing to know that! But in about 500 BC, a Phoenician called Hanno set off on a sightseeing trip along the west African coast where he also hoped to found some settlements. Among the weird and wonderful things he saw were crocodiles, hippos and some very small, very hairy people. Puzzled Hanno didn't know it, but they were probably chimpanzees.

LOOKS LIKE YOUR BROTHER

Still raring to go? What d'ya mean, you're feeling a bit seasick? Go on, push the boat out... You'll be in good company. The famous sailor you're about to meet didn't have time to moan about seasickness. He had enough trouble working out exactly where on Earth he was.

Confused Columbus

In 1492, Christopher Columbus set off on a voyage that changed the whole course of geography. He discovered a brand new part of the world – BY ACCIDENT. Not that he ever admitted it. According to Columbus, he'd been somewhere else at the time. Here's his earth-shattering story...

Horrible Geography Travellers' Tales

Christopher was born in Genoa, Italy. His dad was a wool weaver and the rest of his childhood is a bit, er, woolly. But we do know that, even as a lad, Chris was horribly curious. He wanted to see the big, wide world. He spent all his spare time reading Marco Polo's book and daydreaming of following in his hero's footsteps. It drove his poor mum mad.

When Columbus was 25 years old, he went to Portugal to work as a chart-maker (a chart's a map used at sea). But his heart wasn't really in his work and he longed to be off. Handily, in those days, Portugal was the perfect place for a budding explorer to be. Portuguese ships sailed far and wide, bringing back fabulous riches from the mysterious Indies (the lands we now call Asia). Columbus loved to listen to the salty sailors' extraordinary tales, like the one about the island with beaches covered in gold sand – even though there wasn't a grain of truth in it.

Earth-shattering fact
It was thanks to Prince Henry the Navigator (1394–1460) that Portugal became such a top spot for exploration. But despite his nautical nickname, Prince Henry never actually went to sea himself. Instead he planned loads of daring expeditions to send other people on, including several to Africa. And he set up a school for navigators where all the top Portuguese sailors trained. Apparently, Henry was just following what was written in his horoscope. What a star!

Then, one day, Columbus had a brilliant idea. An idea so earth-shattering it would change the face of the world: rather than sail *east* to the Indies, why not sail *west* instead? OK, so this might not sound very exciting to you, but at the time it was ground-breaking stuff. No one had ever sailed across the Atlantic Ocean before. No one knew if you even could. They called it the "Green Sea of Darkness" and steered well clear.

Across the Atlantic

But first Columbus had to find someone to stump up the cash for his voyage. It was easier said than done. Most people laughed their socks off at his crackpot plan. Fed up with being fobbed off, Columbus fled to Spain where the really rich King and Queen agreed to dish up the dosh.

At last, on 3 August 1492, Columbus set sail from Spain with three ships and 90 sailors and headed west into the unknown. At first, everything went swimmingly. The weather was fine, and gentle winds blew the ships along steadily. But as the days turned into weeks there was still no sight of land. And things started to turn nasty. Very nasty. The sailors pleaded with Columbus to turn back before it was too late. If he didn't, they said, they'd throw him overboard (they didn't actually tell Columbus this bit). But Columbus wasn't about to turn back now. No way.

To keep the suffering sailors' spirits up, Columbus kept an official log (that's a ship's diary, not a piece of wood). He gave it to the crew to read. Here's how it might have gone...

Ships (official) log.
Date: 26 September 1492
To be read by ABSOLUTELY EVERYONE.

Things are going brilliantly. Exactly as I'd planned. We're bang on course, I'm glad to say, and it won't be long before we reach land. We've seen loads of sea birds and everyone knows they never fly far from shore.
Besides, you know what I always say:
"If you sail the seas, you will always find land".
I mean, would I lead you on a wild goose chase? Well, would I?

41

Unfortunately for Columbus, his top-secret log was closer to the terrible truth…

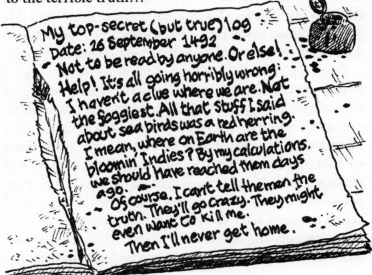

My top-secret (but true) log
Date: 26 September 1492
Not to be read by anyone. Or else!
Help! It's all going horribly wrong!
I haven't a clue where we are. Not
the foggiest. All that stuff I said
about sea birds was a red herring.
I mean, where on Earth are the
bloomin' Indies? By my calculations,
we should have reached them days
ago.
Of course, I can't tell the men the
truth. They'll go crazy. They might
even want to kill me.
Then I'll never get home.

The Indies, or else

Early in the morning of 12 October, the lookout sighted land. At last! After 33 gruelling days at sea, the men couldn't believe their luck. Columbus called the island San Salvador and claimed it for Spain (that's what explorers did in those days).

Horrible geographers reckon the island was in the Bahamas, in the Caribbean Sea. That's off the coast of North and South America.
AND NOWHERE NEAR ASIA.

ATLAS

So Columbus hadn't reached the Indies. He wasn't even close. Did it bother him? Not a bit. He firmly believed he'd reached Asia and he didn't care what anyone said. He even got his confused crew to sign a document going along with his story. Else he'd have their tongues cut out. Nice!

Over the next few months, Columbus set off on an island cruise. What a place for a holiday! Then on Christmas Day, disaster struck. His ship, the *Santa Maria*, ran aground near an island which Columbus called Hispaniola. (He secretly hoped it was Japan. Talk about wishful thinking. Today it's split between the countries of Haiti and the Dominican Republic.) Luckily, the local people were very friendly and helped the shipwrecked sailors ashore. Crafty Columbus built a stout fort from the ship's timbers and left 39 men behind to search for gold. Then he and the others sailed home to Spain in the other two seaworthy ships.

In case he didn't make it back, Columbus wrote a letter to the King and Queen of Spain telling them how brilliant he was. What a bighead. Then he put it in a barrel and chucked it in the sea. Bet that was a barrel of laughs.

In March 1493, Columbus arrived back in Spain, to a hero's welcome. The King and Queen were dead chuffed to see him, especially as he'd brought them piles of top presents. They gave him loads of grand-sounding titles, like "Admiral of the Ocean Sea" (that's the Atlantic to you and me). There was no doubt about it, Columbus had the world at his feet.

Teacher teaser

Columbus was a brilliant sailor. But even brilliant sailors can get it wrong. Is your geography teacher clued-up enough to spot Columbus's BIG MISTAKE?

a) Columbus thought the world was bigger than it actually was.

b) Columbus thought the world was smaller than it actually was.

c) Columbus didn't expect to find any land between Europe and Asia.

Is your teacher all at sea? Why not put him out of his misery and tell him the right answer. He'll be so gobsmacked at your new-found nautical know-how, he might let you off geography homework for a week. Not.

Answer: b) and **c)** OK, so that's two mistakes, but who's counting?

---

b) Columbus knew the Earth was big and round but he hadn't a clue just how big. The truth is, no one did. He tried to work it out but got his maths in a muddle and made the Earth a quarter too small. Which is why the sailors were surprised at how long the vile voyage was taking.

c) The old maps Columbus used showed the Earth covered half in land and half in sea. The ocean stretched right round the world from western Europe to eastern Asia. With nothing in between. That's because no one knew the Americas were there. And that's why they called them the New World, because it was news to them. No wonder Columbus got his wires crossed.

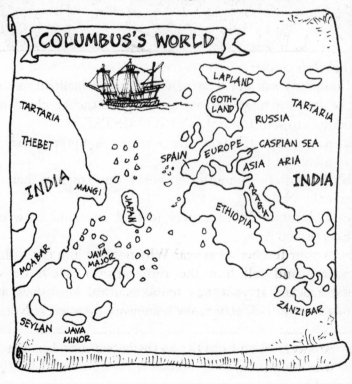

COLUMBUS'S WORLD

LAPLAND
GOTH-LAND
RUSSIA
TARTARIA
TARTARIA
THEBET
SPAIN
EUROPE
CASPIAN SEA
ASIA
ARIA
INDIA
MANGI
JAPAN
ARABIA
INDIA
ETHIOPIA
MOABAR
JAVA MAJOR
ZANZIBAR
SEYLAN
JAVA MINOR

An unhappy ending

Columbus made three more journeys to the New World and explored many more of the islands. But instead of enjoying his hard-won fame, Columbus found that things went horribly wrong. A Spanish judge charged him with being a bad governor of the new lands he'd found and he was sent home in chains. Columbus died in 1506, a bitterly disappointed man. He never felt people gave him the respect he deserved for his intrepid travels. After all, he was the first European to sail the awesome Atlantic. And he'd discovered a New World. Not that he'd ever own up to it.

Earth-shattering fact
Columbus didn't even get his New World named after him. That honour went to top Italian explorer and pickle-seller Amerigo Vespucci (1454–1512). But it wasn't Amerigo's doing. In 1507 a German geographer wrote his name on a map by mistake. He tried to change it later but by then "America" had stuck.

ER... HAVE YOU GOT AN ERASER, HANS?

A strange saga

Ask most geography teachers which European "discovered" America and 99.9% of them will say Columbus, of course. But did he? Some horrible geographers think the adventurous Vikings beat Columbus to it years before. They reckon a Viking called Leif the

Lucky sailed to Newfoundland, on the east coast of Canada, in about AD 1000. Lucky Leif called the place he landed in Vinland ("Wine-land") because of all the grapes growing there.

Not everyone was thrilled to know the New World had been "found". For the locals who'd lived there all along, the explorers' arrival spelled disaster. They brought deadly diseases like smallpox which wiped them out and many of the explorers treated them like slaves. They also stole the locals' land and gold. They wanted to get rich quick. And they didn't care how they did it.

After curious Columbus's extraordinary expedition, exploration really took off. But I bet you can't guess the reason for the next nail-biting voyage. Want a clue? It's something you might put on your disgusting school dinner to disguise the terrible taste…

Magnificent Magellan

Give up? Well, the answer is pepper. Yep, ordinary, everyday pepper you sprinkle on your food. Today we take pepper for granted, but centuries ago in Europe, pepper and other spices were worth their weight in gold. People used them to disguise the putrid taste of gone-off meat. Phwoar! But you couldn't just pop to the shops for them. Explorers had to make horribly long and hazardous journeys to Asia to bring spices back from the Spice Islands (the Moluccas in Indonesia).

Earth-shattering fact
In July 1497, daring Portuguese sailor Vasco da Gama (1460–1524) set off from Lisbon to find a sea route from Europe to Asia. He took with him four ships, 150 men and a handful of prisoners to act as spies. After sailing round the Cape of Good Hope, the southernmost tip of Africa, and across the Indian Ocean, they reached the west coast of India in May 1498 and became the first Europeans ever to sail to India.

WE'LL BE GREETED AS HEROES.

OI! GET OFF MY VEGETABLE PATCH!

Now one of the most intrepid sailors of all is about to set off on a daring adventure. If you're quick, you might just have time to hop on board his ship...

Horrible Geography Travellers' Tales

Ferdinand's mum and dad were posh nobles. And they had big plans for their boy. When he was 12, they sent him to court in Lisbon to be a page to the Queen. Ferdinand got to learn music, hunting and sword-fighting. It sounds like a pretty ace life for a young lad but Ferdinand wasn't happy. He longed to go to sea.

Some years later, Ferdie got his chance and joined the King's fleet of ships. He quickly got himself promoted to captain and sailed all the way east to the Spice Islands and the Philippines, following in Vasco da Gama's footsteps. On one expedition, he got wounded in battle and from then on always walked with a limp.

Spicing things up a bit

In 1519, Magellan set sail on his most daring voyage so far. Instead of sailing east like da Gama, he wanted to reach the Spice Islands by sailing west instead. There was just one tiny snag. South America lay in his way and no one knew if there was a way round it. Some people claimed to have heard of *el paso* (that's Spanish for "the passage"), a channel of water leading from the Atlantic Ocean through South America and into the sea beyond. But nobody knew for sure. Meanwhile, Magellan had other things on his mind. He was desperately short of cash. And without cash, he was going nowhere. Then he fell out with the King of Portugal and had to move to Spain. Luckily, King Charles I of Spain liked Magellan and agreed to pay for the whole trip (any excuse to get one up on his arch rivals, the Portuguese). So, on 20 September 1519, Magellan at last set sail with five ships (including his own ship, the *Trinidad*) and 280 men.

Here's how Magellan might have described his voyage in his letters home to his wife, Beatriz:

The Trinidad, Rio de Janeiro, Brazil
December 1519

My dearest Beatriz,
I hope this letter reaches you safely. The voyage has been FANTASTIC so far. Well, bits of it anyway. When we left Spain, we headed south-west across the Atlantic. So far, so good, I thought. Then the weather turned nasty. Really nasty. We were battered by terrible storms, then guess what? The wind died down completely so we drifted round and round in circles, going nowhere fast! Then the sun came out and it was blazing hot. The food started to go rotten and the tar holding the ships' timbers together melted in the heat so the ships kept springing leaks.

Brazil
we are here →x

PTO →

Anyway, we've been in Rio for a week now
and had the ships fixed. And what a brilliant
place it is. The locals are so friendly and can't
do enough for us. The crew are having the time
of their lives - they've never had it so good.
Of course, I'm much too busy with my
charts to join in the partying.

    Missing you loads,
    Love,
    Ferdie xx

The Trinidad, Patagonia, South America
April 1520

Dear Beatriz,
What a few months it's been! We left Rio on
Christmas Day - there wasn't a dry eye on
deck, I can tell you. And no wonder. As we
sailed south, the seas got stormier and the
winds were bitter. The crew began to
grumble, and things started to take a turn
for the worse. You see, the men wanted to
head back to Rio, but I told them, like it or
lump it, we were continuing south. There was
no turning back.

    By the end of March, I'd had enough of
their bickering. We dropped anchor in a little
harbour called San Julian where I've decided
to spend the winter.* I was looking forward to

pto →

51

a good rest but just as I thought things were calming down, three of the ships' captains went and started a mutiny! It's true they've never liked me, but I didn't think they'd go this far. I had to act fast. I had two of them beheaded, and the other marooned. I know it sounds cruel, dear, but they'd really gone and done it this time.

Please don't worry about me, dear. I'll be fine.

Love,
Ferdie xx

*In the southern hemisphere, the seasons are the other way round. So when it's summer up north, it's winter down south, and the other way round.

The Trinidad, the Straits of Magellan, South America
October 1520

Dearest Beatriz,
We've found it! We've found it! Oh, yippee! I'm sooo happy! A few weeks ago, a terrible storm blew two of the ships towards the rocks. I'd given them up for lost, but then the most amazing thing happened. I still can't quite believe it. Suddenly, I saw the ships in the distance, sails billowing.

PTO →

The wind had blown them into a channel of water lined with high cliffs. Yes, dear, they'd found el paso and seen sea on the other side! I must admit, Beatriz dear, I had a lump in my throat. (But don't tell anyone)

I named the passage, well, after me. The Straits of Magellan! It's got a ring to it, hasn't it? It took us a month to sail through but it was well worth the wait. On the other side lay a vast ocean as far as the eye could see. It's so calm and peaceful, dear, I've called it the Pacific Ocean.

Straits of Magellan

Pacific Ocean

Atlantic Ocean

Wish you were here.
Love,
Ferdie xx

The Trinidad, somewhere in Pacific Ocean
February 1521

Dear Beatriz,
Sorry about the shaky writing. I'm not feeling very well. We've been sailing across this wretched ocean for months now and there's not been a glimpse of land. The Pacific, pah! How wrong can you be? I'm beginning to hate the place. We've got nothing to drink but a few sips of stinking, scummy water (it's OK if you hold your nose). And nothing to eat but stale currant biscuits (actually the currants are really rat poo but

PTO→

53

I haven't told the men. Sometimes we have sawdust soup or boiled rat which makes a nice change. But the men are dropping like flies from scurvy* or they're too weak to move. I don't know how long we can go on like this.

Love,
Ferdie xx

Horrible Health Warning
You can read more about scurvy later on (page 64). But don't do it while you're eating. It might put you off your tea...

The Trinidad, the Philippines
April 1521

Dearest Bea,
Just when I thought we were done for, we sighted a beautiful tropical island ahead. Safe at last. What a relief! We had just about enough strength left to row to the shore. Then we scoffed down a fabulous feast of fish, bananas and coconuts. Yummy! It's the first fresh food we've had for ages.

Dinner

PtO →

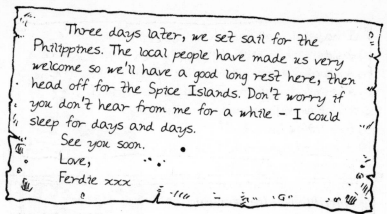

Three days later, we set sail for the Philippines. The local people have made us very welcome so we'll have a good long rest here, then head off for the Spice Islands. Don't worry if you don't hear from me for a while – I could sleep for days and days.

See you soon.

Love,

Ferdie xxx

A sticky end

But Beatriz never saw her husband again. On 27 April, Magellan was killed in a fight between two warring islands. Juan Sebastian del Cano, an ex-mutineer, took command of the expedition. He sailed to the Spice Islands, filled the ships with valuable cloves and then began the long journey home.

On 6 September 1522, an utter wreck of a ship sailed home to Spain. It was the *Victoria*, the only ship left of the five that had set sail three years earlier. Only 18 suffering sailors out of the 280 who'd left Spain had survived the odious ordeal. They'd sailed 85,000 kilometres and become the first Europeans to cross the perilous Pacific and sail right around the world. A truly intrepid feat.

Magellan was dead unlucky. Not only was he dead, of course, which was unlucky for him, but for years his amazing achievements (after all, the whole thing had been his bright idea) were ignored and creepy del Cano got all the credit.

Could you be a suffering sailor?

Could you have been a sailor in Magellan's time? Try this quick quiz to find out. If you think you've suffered enough, get your geography teacher to try it instead.

1 What would you wear?
a) A smart white uniform.
b) A set of waterproof overalls.
c) A smock, baggy trousers and a woolly hat.
2 Where would you sleep?
a) In a comfy bunk bed.
b) Anywhere you could find space.
c) In a hammock on deck.
3 Where would you go to the toilet?
a) Over the side of the ship.
b) In a bucket on board.
c) In a bathroom with a flush toilet.

Answers:

1c) Sailors didn't care about being trendy. Their clothes were big and baggy so they could move about and work easily. And they weren't that bothered about keeping clean. Ships didn't have washing machines. So if your clothes got drenched or dirty, you just had to pong.

2b) Sorry, you only got to sleep on a bed if you were a high-up ship's officer. And then it wasn't really a bed at all, just a lumpy pile of mouldy old straw. Ordinary sailors kipped wherever they could find a space. And you could forget about having a long lie-in. You had to wake up every four hours to take your turn at keeping watch. You'd be flogged if you forgot.

3a) Yep, I'm afraid it's true. There was a plank you could sit on but it was horribly hazardous especially if the weather was bad. But many sailors didn't bother walking the plank. They went in the bilge instead (a layer of stinking water below deck that helped to balance the boat). You needed a strong stomach – the smell was unspeakable.

Earth-shattering fact

A part-time pirate led the second expedition successfully to sail around the world. In December 1577, swashbuckling English sailor Francis Drake (1543–1596) set off from Plymouth, England. His official instructions from Queen Elizabeth I herself were to claim new lands for England. But secretly she wanted him to plunder Spanish ships full of priceless treasure from South America. (Spain was England's arch enemy at that time.) Which is precisely what dashing Drake did. By the time he returned home three years later, his ships were crammed full of rich pickings – gold, silver, pearls, silk, posh china and spices. No wonder the Queen was pleased. She rewarded him with a knighthood and his fame and fortune were guaranteed.

If a sailor's life sounds too sickening, why not leave it to an expert instead? Like the brilliant sailor in the next section. He wasn't interested in money or trade routes, though. Nope, he wanted to see the world and learn more about horrible geography. Hard to believe, I know.

Courageous Cook

Top British sailor James Cook was undoubtedly intrepid and brave. In the eighteenth century, he led three of the greatest voyages of exploration ever made. Not bad for a lad from a humble family who started off selling fruit and veg.

Horrible Geography Travellers' Tales

JAMES COOK
(1728-1779)
NATIONALITY:
BRITISH

James was born in England. His dad worked on a farm and his dad's boss paid for young James to go to school. When James was 12, he went to work in a grocer's shop. But he didn't give a fig about boring fruit and veg and got a job on a coal ship. Later, he joined the British Royal Navy and was promoted to lieutenant. In his spare time, James managed to teach himself maths and surveying. What a swot! Everyone said he was a brilliant sailor and a born leader. Which is why, in 1768, he was picked to lead a daring new scientific expedition to the far-flung South Pacific.

Earth-shattering fact
The first expedition to set sail in the name of science rather than trade was led by French navigator and mathematician Louis-Antoine de Bougainville (1729–1811). In 1766, two years before Cook set off, he left France with a boatload of scientists to sail around the world. He was gone for two years. But he returned with hundreds of specimens of amazing new plants and animals, including a beautiful bloomer from South America which was named bougainvillea in his honour.

THIS IS BLOOMIN' MARVELLOUS!

First voyage (1768–1771)
The Navy wanted Cook to watch the planet Venus as it moved across the face of the sun. This was important for measuring the distance between the Earth and the sun, and for making navigation more accurate. Trouble was, this cosmic combination only happened twice every 100 years. So it was crucial to be in the right place at the right time. And the right place in 1769 turned out to be the island of Tahiti in the South Pacific Ocean.

At least, those were the official plans... Burning a hole in his coat pocket, however, Cook had an envelope marked TOP SECRET. Inside were top-secret orders from the British Government which curious Cook wasn't allowed to read until he reached Tahiti. Don't worry, you won't have to wait that long. Here's a sneak preview. But, ssh ... don't tell anyone.

TOP-SECRET (OFFICIAL) ORDERS
To: Lieutenant James Cook
Your top-secret mission:

You are to proceed to the south-ward in order to make discovery of the Southern Continent, unless you sooner fall in with it.
But not having discovered it or any evident signs of it, you are to proceed in search of it to the westward until you discover it, or fall in with the coast of New Zealand.

Signed
The British Government

P.S. Then you can come home.
P.P.S. Don't tell anyone about this. Or else!

What on Earth was this Southern Continent and where on Earth was it? And exactly why was it such a big secret? Here's Miles to spill the beans.

It's actually Antarctica. The Ancient Greeks guessed Antarctica existed though they'd never actually been there. They reckoned there must be a big chunk of land in the south to balance the big chunk in the north. On early maps, it was labelled Terra Australis Incognita, which means "unknown southern land". But it was so far away that for centuries no Europeans were keen to go looking for it. Now that many of the gaps in the map had been filled in, explorers (and governments) turned their sights south. And now the race was well and truly on to see who could find the mysterious continent first.

An epic voyage
In August 1768, Cook set sail on the *Endeavour*, a sturdy coal ship. On board were 97 men, including a whole bunch of boring scientists.

Earth-shattering fact
One of the scientists was top British botanist (a scientist who studies plants) Joseph Banks (1743–1820). When he wasn't being seasick, he spent his time leafing through botany books and collecting thousands of new types of plants. (He took along four servants to help him sort the specimens out.) Banks was also the first scientist from Europe to see a kangaroo. He must have jumped with joy! Then he shot it and ate it for his tea. Anyone for a kangaroo sandwich?

After a horribly hard and dangerous journey, the *Endeavour* reached Tahiti in April 1769. Even the suffering scientists perked up a bit. They built an observatory and unpacked their telescopes and instruments. Then, on 3 June, the moment they'd been waiting for arrived at last. The weather was perfect and they watched in amazement as Venus moved across the sun. Cosmic! It was so incredibly exciting Cook almost forgot the crumpled envelope in his pocket. His hands trembled as he read its secret contents...

There was no time to lose. In July, the *Endeavour* set sail again and headed south. And further south. But there was no sign of any secret Southern Continent. Instead, Cook kept the crew busy drawing up brand-new maps of Australia and New Zealand. It was a long, painstaking job. Then, in June the following year, disaster struck. The *Endeavour* hit a coral reef which gashed a gaping hole in its side. Quick-thinking Cook patched the ship up with a spare sail and a load of, er, sheep's poo. Then he managed to sail to Indonesia where it was repaired.

On 12 July 1771, the *Endeavour* finally made it home after three thrilling years at sea. True, Cook hadn't discovered a new continent, but he had visited places never seen before and earned his place in the geography books. He was given a hero's welcome and a well-earned promotion.

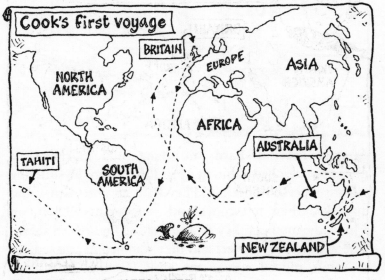

Second voyage (1772–1775)

It wasn't long before Cook was off again with two new ships to search for the Southern Continent. It was a truly treacherous trip. As they sailed further and further south, the weather turned bitterly cold and the sea was littered with lethal icebergs. One false move in the thick fog and the ships would have been scuppered. All this left crestfallen Cook convinced that there was no way Antarctica could exist. And, even if it did, there was no way anyone could reach it. Dejectedly, he wrote in his diary:

> I had now made the circuit of the Southern Ocean ... and traversed it in such a manner as to leave not the least room for the possibility of there being a continent, unless near the Pole and out of reach of Navigation.

He saw no reason, he added, why anyone should want to sail in these cold and dangerous waters again. Nope, Antarctica definitely wasn't top of his list of places to go on his holidays. Back home, Cook tried to take his mind off things by writing a paper about scurvy...

Horrible Health Warning
Scurvy was a dreadful disease suffered by sailors. It was caused by not eating enough vital Vitamin C (found in fresh fruit and veg). Its sickening symptoms began with your gums swelling up so your teeth fell out when you tried to eat. Then you grew woefully weak and ill, and died a painful death. Caring Cook devised a cunning plan for keeping the deadly disease at bay. He made his unfortunate crew scoff platefuls of ... pickled cabbage. And you thought school dinners were bad. (Another crazy cure was to rub your gums with wee.) Later, it was found that drinking lemon or lime juice did the trick. Now, come on, eat up your greens!

Third voyage (1776–1779)

For his third voyage, Cook planned to search for a sea route across the top of North America. Things started off swimmingly. Instead of a boring sea route, he discovered the idyllic holiday islands of Hawaii.

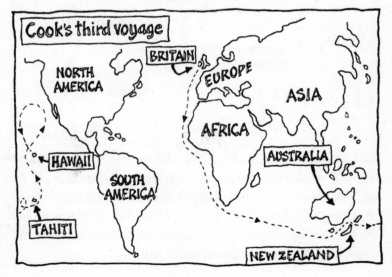

Cook's third voyage

The Hawaiians were very friendly and declared Cook a god. But even gods can outstay their welcome, especially if food is running short. After months on the island, the locals were fed up with the sailors and wanted them to leave. On 14 February 1779, Cook was stabbed and killed in a bad-tempered skirmish on the beach. His body was buried at sea.

Earth-shattering fact
Amazingly, clever Cook was the first sailor to know where on Earth he was. This was thanks to a brilliant new device called a marine chronometer (kron-om-eater). It was invented by English clock-maker John Harrison and was like a clock for measuring longitude (how far east or west you were). If you knew your longitude and your latitude (how far north or south you were), you could pinpoint exactly where you were on the globe. Pity suffering sailors couldn't do this before.

Horrible geographers agree that Cook was the most intrepid sailor of his day. His pioneering voyages covered thousands of kilometres and opened up vast parts of the world. But have you seen enough of the sea? Do you fancy going somewhere hot and sunny? Somewhere so scorching it'll fry your brains and drive you mad with thirst. Don't forget to pack the sun cream. You'll need it where we're off to next.

DESERT DISCOVERERS

Welcome to the desperate desert. How's this for a change of scene? Within minutes of arriving, you might wish you were back at sea. You'll be horribly hot and bothered and dying for a drink. Even the local people have a tough time keeping their cool. So why on Earth would intrepid explorers risk being fried alive in this place? Again, some of them wanted to open the desert up for trade and settlement. But others had heard rumours of fabled desert cities and wanted to visit them for themselves. They didn't worry about the danger. What danger? Talk about sticking your head in the sand.

Horrible Health Warning

The dreadful desert heat, and the lack of food and water, can drive even the hardiest explorer barking mad. Take intrepid French explorer, René Caillié (1799–1838). In 1827, René set off to cross the deadly Sahara Desert in Africa. Here's what he said about his appalling ordeal:

I was reduced to extremity. My eyes were hollow, I panted for breath, and my tongue hung out of my mouth. I recollect that at every halt, I fell to the ground from weakness, and had not even the strength to eat... I was not, however, the worst off, for I saw several drink their own urine.

Intrepid Ibn Battutah

Ibn Battutah's motto was "Never travel the same road twice". Sounds adventurous, doesn't it? But this must have made it horribly difficult for him to find his way back home.

Horrible Geography Travellers' Tales

Ibn Battutah was born in Tangier, Morocco. He must have had a good education because he trained to be a judge. Battutah was a devout Muslim (a person who follows the religion of Islam), and when he was 21, he threw his bags on a camel and set off across the desert to Arabia. He wanted to visit Mecca, the Muslims' holiest city. It was a trip that changed his life. On the way Battutah met a wise old man who dreamed Ibn would be a great explorer. He must have been a good judge of character.

Earth-shattering fact
Ibn Battutah's full name was Abu Abd Allah Muhammad Ibn Abd Allah Al-Lawati Attanji Ibn Battutah. What a mouthful! By the time he'd introduced himself to people he met on his travels, they'd got bored and gone off to talk to someone else.

A good judge of names

Ibn Battutah was well and truly bitten by the exploring bug. For 30 years he was hardly ever at home. On his way to Mecca he popped into Egypt and Syria. Then he crossed the dusty Arabian Desert to Persia and Iraq. Next, he hopped on a ship and sailed down the east coast of Africa as far as exotic Zanzibar. You name it, he went there. His feet barely touched the ground. He must have spent a fortune on postcards home.

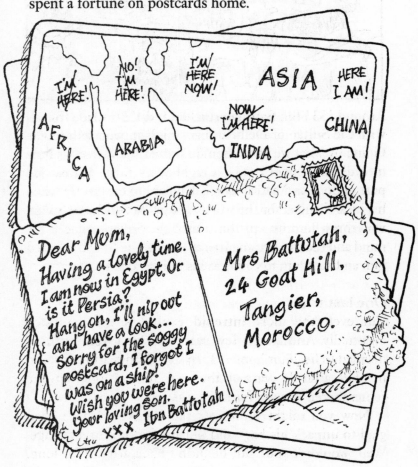

Everywhere Ibn Battutah went, he was treated like an honoured guest and soon his name was on everyone's lips...

Around 1333 Ibn Battutah reached India. He made friends with the Sultan of Delhi and got a job at court as a judge. Going by what we know from his notes, he was very happy in India and spent the next eight years there. He earned pots of dosh and had a big, posh palace to live in. But then his luck changed for the worse. He fell out with the Sultan who threw him into prison. Later, the Sultan changed his mind and the two became friends again. The Sultan released him and sent him to China as his official ambassador.

One last trip
But even the most intrepid explorers get homesick eventually. And after a few years in China, Ibn Battutah decided to head for home. He reached Tangier in Morocco in 1349, after 24 years on the road. It's a wonder anyone remembered who on Earth he was...

Now you might think intrepid Ibn would have been glad to unpack his bags and put his feet up for a change. Well, wouldn't you? But he didn't hang around for long.

71

There was one place he still hadn't visited and he had a burning desire to go. So in 1351 he set off again ... for the scorching Sahara Desert. After crossing the Atlas Mountains he hitched a lift with a camel caravan for the long trek across the desert. It was horribly hard going. The sand stung his eyes and got up his nose, and he was driven mad with thirst.

Could old Battutah stand the heat? You bet he could. On his action-packed trip, he spent a year in the Kingdom of Mali (in west Africa), canoed down the River Niger and visited the legendary desert city of Timbuktu.

By the time he reached home again in 1354, he'd travelled over 120,000 kilometres on his various trips. He spent the rest of his life writing a book and trying to remember where on Earth he'd been... And in case you're having trouble keeping track, don't worry – here's Miles with a handy map of his travels...

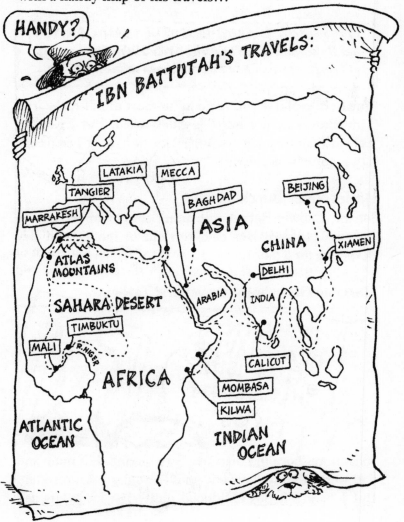

73

Earth-shattering fact
For years, the city of Timbuktu had tantalized travellers. It had been a centre of desert trade for centuries and tales of its fabulous wealth spread far and wide. But until the nineteenth century no one from Europe had ever been there… and come back alive. In 1826, dashing British soldier Alexander Gordon Laing (1793–1826) managed to reach Timbuktu, but he'd hardly set foot in the city when a local chief accused him of being a spy and had him murdered in his sleep.

The next explorer you're going to meet didn't make it to Timbuktu – he got horribly sidetracked. But he didn't feel hard done by. He discovered his own, long-lost desert city – quite by accident.

Undercover Burckhardt

Johann Ludwig Burckhardt didn't set out to become an intrepid explorer. But he'd run out of money and was desperate for a job.

Horrible Geography Travellers' Tales

JOHANN BURCKHARDT (1784-1817) NATIONALITY: SWISS

Johann was born in Lausanne, Switzerland. His mum and dad were quite well off and spoiled young Johann rotten. But Johann's happy childhood didn't last long. His dad lost all his money and was thrown into prison. Later, Johann went off to university but he wasn't very good at studying. He was too busy going to wild parties and getting into fights.

A lucky break

In 1806, penniless Johann sailed to England to look for a job. For months, he couldn't find one and almost starved. Then, one day, his luck changed... A few years before, a group of top London geographers had set up an association for exploring Africa. They desperately needed a volunteer to search for the source of the River Niger. (Everyone they'd sent so far had died or gone missing.) And they were willing to pay £1 a day. Johann desperately needed the cash and, when he was offered the job, he jumped at the chance. His mission sounded simple: to travel to Cairo in Egypt, then across the Sahara Desert to Timbuktu and on to the Niger. But this was to be no holiday.

For the next few months, Johann didn't have time to worry about the risks. He began to learn Arabic (the language spoken in the Middle East and north Africa) and got into training for the desert by walking miles in the midday heat (without a hat) and living on a diet of water and veg. Yuk!

Everything was ready. Well, almost. There was just one big-ish snag. At that time, in the Middle East and Africa, most travellers were Arabs. Europeans like Johann were few and far between, and ran the risk of being robbed or even killed as spies. There was only one thing for it – Johann would have to travel in disguise. And only one disguise would do the trick. He dressed up as an Arab, in a long, flowing robe and long, flowing headdress.

Then, at last, in March 1809, Johann finally hit the road.

Did Johann make it to the Niger? Or did the locals see through his disguise? Where better to read about Johann's daring desert journey than in these extracts from his secret diary? By the way, you'll have to excuse the terrible handwriting. Johann had to keep his notes hidden under his robes, otherwise he'd have blown his disguise.

My Desert Diary

TOP SECRET

By Ibrahim Ibn Abdullah*

*That's the Arabic name Johann used on his travels.

September 1810, Aleppo, Syria

I reached Syria in July 1809 so I've been here for over a year so far. And things are going better than I ever dared to hope. My disguise has held up brilliantly. There was just one sticky moment when a suspicious local tried to pull my beard. A very close shave. I've been practising really hard and I can now speak Arabic pretty fluently, and my Swiss accent's almost gone. I've also made three short trips into the nearby desert to get into training for my journey. I had a bit of bad luck on the third trip, though. I was set on by robbers who stole my money and my camel. Fortunately, they didn't pinch my diary – I'd hidden it in my pants!

my beard

July 1812, the Jordan Valley

With all preparations complete, I left Aleppo in spring 1812 and set off on horseback along the Jordan Valley. Cairo, here I come! I decided to take a roundabout route so I could see a bit more of the countryside. Of course, I knew it was dangerous. The road was lined with piles of stones which marked the graves of travellers who'd been murdered by bandits. Grim. But I reckoned it was worth the risk. At night, I usually found a room in a village hut or tent, and slept on the floor like the locals. And so far, no one's seen through my disguise.

19 August 1812, somewhere in the desert
It's been tough going, I can tell you. The weather's been baking hot, the road's rocky and rough, and the flies are enough to drive you mad. I was glad to reach the town of Kerek where I had a good, long rest. While I was there, I heard a rumour about the ruins of an ancient city hidden in the nearby desert hills. I was desperate to have a look. But finding a guide for the rest of the journey has been trickier than I thought. I finally found one who was willing to take me all the way to Cairo for 20 piastres (£1) and four goats. Daylight robbery. Still, there's no point bleating on about it.

22 August 1812, Petra, Jordan
What a day! I was determined to see the ruined city but if I'd made a sudden detour it would have made my guide suspicious. So I pretended that I wanted to sacrifice a goat in honour of the prophet

Haroun. His tomb lay at the end of the valley and we'd have to pass through the city to reach it. Cunning, eh? But my heart was in my mouth. I followed the guide through a narrow winding gorge and suddenly there it was! A magnificent, ancient city, carved out of the rose-red desert rock! I managed to sneak a peek at the exquisite buildings and tombs. But the guide was getting twitchy and I dared not stay too long. I just had a chance to scribble loads of notes, then it was time to leave.

Johann had stumbled on the ruins of the ancient city of Petra. In the first century BC, it was the capital of the flourishing Nabatean Empire. The Nabateans were nomads from western Arabia who grew rich plundering passing trading caravans. Later, Petra was taken over by the Romans, but in the seventh century AD it fell into decline. Johann was the first European to see the city that had lain forgotten for 1,000 years. It was an incredible find.

Waiting for a caravan

From Petra, Johann carried on his journey to Cairo and reached it in September 1812. His plan was to join a caravan to take him across the Sahara Desert to Timbuktu, where he could start his exploration of the Niger River. (After all, that was the reason he'd come all this way.) But weeks passed, and no caravans showed up. Restless Johann soon got bored of sitting around all day and twiddling his thumbs. Still in disguise, he went on a sightseeing tour of Egypt, then made a pilgrimage to Mecca in Arabia (the Muslims' holy city). (It's just as well his disguise held up. Non-Muslims were forbidden to enter Mecca – on pain of death.)

In January 1815, Johann caught a fever and cut his travels short. After a long and hazardous journey, he returned to Cairo ... to wait for the next caravan to Africa. Sadly, the caravan never came and, two years later, Johann fell ill and died. He never made it to Timbuktu or got to navigate the Niger. Instead, undercover Johann had uncovered one of the greatest of all desert discoveries.

Earth-shattering fact

Brave Burckhardt wasn't the only desert discoverer to travel in disguise. In 1853, fearless British explorer Richard Burton (1821–1890) followed in Johann's footsteps and sneaked into Mecca, dressed as a Muslim doctor. (He wasn't really a doctor but he made quite a name for himself when he IT'S ME! WHO? *cured two people of snoring.) In fact, his disguise was so convincing it even fooled his friends. When he later turned up in Cairo, none of them recognized him.*

Meanwhile, on the other side of the world, explorers were trying to solve the mystery of what lay in the middle of Australia. Was it fields of fertile farmland, a gently lapping lake, or scorching, bone-dry desert?

Suffering Stuart

John McDouall Stuart didn't look much like an intrepid explorer. He was small and slightly built and didn't look as if he'd say "Boo" to a goose, let alone set off on a wild-goose chase...

Horrible Geography Travellers' Tales

John was born in Scotland but, as a young man, he emigrated to Australia where he worked as a farmer and a surveyor (someone who measures and maps pieces of land). He arrived in Adelaide, South Australia, in January 1839. At that time, people still had no idea what the inside of

Australia was like. There was only one way to find out –
someone would have to cross the continent and see for
themselves. The South Australian government offered a large
cash prize to the first European expedition to cross from the
south to the north coast. But it was easier said than done.

Earth-shattering fact
*In 1844, explorer Charles
Sturt led the first attempt to
cross Australia. What a pity
that Sturt (1795–1869)
picked the hottest summer for
years. He and his companions
were forced to dig holes in the
ground to shelter from the
blazing sun. It was so hot*

I THINK I'M READY FOR IT NOW.

*that Sturt couldn't write his expedition diary because the
ink dried up as soon as it left his pen. When the rains
finally broke, Sturt plodded grimly on. But the
sweltering heat forced him back just 250 kilometres from
the centre. On the wretched return trip, across the
waterless desert wastes, suffering Sturt went blind, was
burnt to a crisp and had to be carried on a stretcher
because he was too weak to walk.*

Crossing the continent

Stuart might have looked feeble and frail but don't be fooled
by looks. He was Sturt's assistant on his epic trip and was
already an experienced traveller. Besides, he was brilliant
at living in the bush and hated sleeping indoors. Sturt's
expedition changed Stuart's life. He gave up surveying for
good and took up exploring instead. He wanted to succeed
where Sturt had failed, and cross Australia.

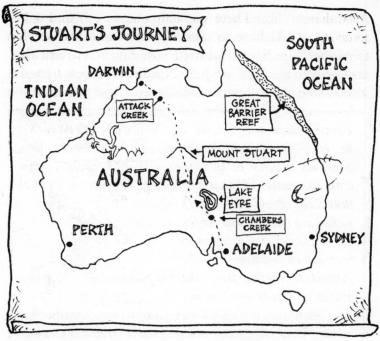

- First expedition
  In August 1859, stout-hearted Stuart, three companions
  and 12 horses set off from Adelaide to cross the
  continent. They travelled north to Chambers Creek,
  then on to Lake Eyre, and headed north-west, crossing
  the Macdonnell Ranges (which he named after the
  governor of South Australia). In April 1860, they
  reached the centre of Australia at last. And guess what
  they found there? Yep – red, dry, dusty desert. Stuart
  was the first European to see this scorching sight. He
  wrote in his diary:

Today I find from my observation ... that I am now
camped in the centre of Australia.

83

To celebrate, he and his companions climbed a hill (they called it Mount Sturt but it was later renamed Mount Stuart) and planted a flag on top. Then they pushed on. But in June, disaster struck. They'd travelled a gruelling 2,400 kilometres and were just 500 kilometres from the north coast. But supplies were running low and Stuart was suffering horribly from scurvy. To make matters worse, unfriendly locals blocked their way (at a place Stuart named Attack Creek), forcing them to turn back. Exhausted and half-starving, they reached Adelaide in August where suffering Stuart was given a hero's welcome.

- Second expedition
  The following January, Stuart set off again from his base camp at Chambers Creek. This time, he took 12 men and 49 horses along for the ride. It was horribly hard going. The baking heat sapped their strength and there was never enough to eat or drink.

At Attack Creek, they spent days desperately trying to clear a path through the miles of thick, thorny bushes that lay between them and the sea. But by July, Stuart had to admit defeat and, bitterly disappointed, he headed home again.

- Third expedition

Not that Stuart was put off. He was more determined than ever to reach his goal and, in October 1861, he left Adelaide again on his third intrepid expedition. But would it be third time lucky for our hopeful hero? The expedition was called "The South Australian Great Northern Exploring Expedition". And, you'll be pleased to know, it lived up to its grand-sounding name. This time, by slightly altering their course, Stuart and his men found a way round the bush. And on 24 July 1862, a delighted Stuart wrote in his diary:

Stopped the horses to clear a way, whilst I advanced a few yards on to the beach, and was gratified and delighted to behold the water of the Indian Ocean in Van Diemen's Gulf... I returned to the valley, where I had my initials cut on a large tree.

Nine months after leaving Adelaide, he'd reached the sea at long last, near the site of the modern-day city of Darwin. He and his sore-footed men gave three cheers, then hobbled into the sea for a quick paddle.

Stuart had finally done it – he'd crossed Australia. But the hardship he had suffered took a terrible toll on his health. Almost blind and barely able to speak, he had to be carried most of the way back to Adelaide in a makeshift sling slung between two of the horses. Utterly worn out, he and his weary men arrived in Adelaide in December, and were greeted by cheering crowds. Sadly, Stuart's superhuman efforts had sapped his strength and he died soon afterwards.

His trail-blazing trip had proved once and for all that most of Australia was baking, barren desert. And a few years later, an overland telegraph line was laid along the route he'd opened up between Adelaide and Darwin. From there, an undersea cable linked Australia to the rest of the world. All thanks to Stuart's guts and determination.

Earth-shattering fact
Long-suffering Stuart wasn't actually the first to cross the continent. A rival expedition, led by Robert O'Hara Burke (1820–1861) and William John Wills (1834–1861), beat him to it. Burke and Wills reached the Gulf of Carpentaria in February 1861. But, unlike Stuart, they didn't make it back. Exhausted and starving, they died on their return journey at their camp at Cooper's Creek. Tragically, they'd missed the rescue party waiting at the camp by just a few hours.

But enough of this doom and gloom. To cheer you up, the next sizzling story's about an intrepid desert explorer who survived against the odds – thanks to his clucky, sorry, lucky chickens.

Heroic Hedin

The Takla Makan Desert in China is a desperate place to be. Locals call it the "Sea of Death". So you get the picture. But ace explorer Sven Hedin wasn't put off by a name. Crossing the murderous Takla Makan was Sven's burning ambition.

Horrible Geography Travellers' Tales

SVEN HEDIN
(1865-1952)
NATIONALITY:
SWEDISH

Sven's dad was a top architect and he probably wanted young Sven to follow in his footsteps. But Sven didn't do brilliantly at school. He was too busy doing other things, like drawing maps on the dining-room table.

When he left school, lucky Sven got a job as a teacher in Russia. OK, so this might not be your idea of luck but Sven had never left Sweden before and he was desperate to see the world. After this, Sven's feet never touched the ground – he was always on the road. Then, in 1894, he set off on his most daring trip so far, across the treacherous Takla Makan Desert.

The March of Death

When Hedin got back, he was invited to give lots of lectures about his desert travels and thousands of people came to hear him talk. His lectures were so gripping, his audience really felt they were there. Do you fancy coming along to one?

Ladies and Gentlemen... I set out on 10 April from the town of Merket on the edge of the Takla Makan Desert. I was eager to be off. It had taken weeks to round up eight strong camels and to find four men who knew the desert well enough to act as guides. The locals begged us not to go. They were afraid we wouldn't come back from the "Sea of Death" alive.

My plan was to head for the Khotan River in the middle of the Takla Makan. I reckoned it would take a month. And at first we made steady progress. All round us the landscape became more desolate as each day passed. There was no sign of life to be seen and no sound, bar the tinkling of the camel bells. We were getting deeper and deeper into the desert. Soon there would be no turning back. Ten days out, we came to a rare waterhole, surrounded by lush, green grass. I ordered the water bottles to be filled, confident the river was only four days away. Then we headed east into the desert. Now there was only sand as far as the eye could see, piled high in towering dunes. Suddenly a savage sandstorm blew up. Howling winds hurled the sand into the air. Stinging sand got into our mouths, noses, ears and clothes – everywhere.

SSSH!

THAT HAPPENED TO ME AT THE BEACH ONCE.

By now we should have reached the river, but I wasn't too alarmed. By my reckoning we had enough water to last at least another week. Or so I thought. When I looked closer, I discovered the terrible truth. The bottles hadn't been filled properly at the last stop. Even with strict rationing, there was only enough water left for two more days. We tried to dig a well but it turned out to be dry. If we didn't reach the river soon, we would surely die. The men were petrified, needless to say. They muttered about how the desert witches had put a spell on us. I couldn't help but agree. Two days and another sandstorm later, and the last of our water was gone. We were so thirsty we killed the chickens and a sheep and drank their blood. But it didn't keep us going for long. We even drank the brandy we'd brought to fuel the stove. But it just made us sick. One by one, most of the men and camels lay down and died, until only a guide, Kasim, and I were able to continue. By now we were woefully weak and we knew we couldn't survive for long. We staggered on for another day, half-walking, half-crawling across the sand. Just when Kasim could go no further, a miracle happened...

Over the next sand dune, I spotted a green line of trees. I couldn't believe my eyes. We'd reached the Khotan River at last and, against all the odds, we'd been saved! I knelt in the river and drank until I felt my strength return. Then I filled my boots with water and went back to poor Kasim. Together, Kasim and I set out to find help. And, as luck would have it, the very next day, we ran into a group of shepherds who gave us food and shelter. Four days later, one of the men we'd given up for dead turned up safe and well, leading the only camel left alive. They'd been found by travellers and miraculously revived. Between us we'd managed to cross the world's deadliest desert and complete our March of Death. But we'd paid a very high price.

Teacher teaser

Has your teacher been paying attention? Or has he nodded off? Tap him gently on the shoulder (GENTLY, I said) and ask him this thirst-quenching question.

What does your hot and bothered teacher reply?
a) The audience booed and hissed.
b) The audience gave Hedin a standing ovation.
c) The audience rushed out to get a drink.

Answer: c) It's true! Sven painted such a horribly life-like picture of the desperate desert that it left his audience gasping for a drink. After the lecture was over, they rushed out of the room and headed straight for the nearest tap.

Earth-shattering fact
Desperate deserts are full of surprises. As Hungarian-born explorer Mark Aurel Stein (1862–1943) found out. On a trek through the Gobi Desert in 1907, he stumbled on a crumbling cave. It didn't look much from the outside but it turned out to be crammed full of priceless ancient manuscripts, carvings and paintings, perfectly preserved in the dry desert air. They'd been hidden there by Buddhist monks about 900 years before.

Can't stand the desert heat? Getting bogged down in all that sand? Don't worry – there are plenty of other perilous places on Earth just waiting to be explored. If you've got a head for heights, why not check out the monstrous mountains in the next hair-raising section? It'll have you clinging on for dear life.

CRAZY CLIMBERS

People have been climbing mountains for years and years. In fact, you could say mountaineering's as old as the hills. But people didn't start off climbing simply to admire the views. Climbing was a means to an end. Mountains often reared their ugly heads in the middle of an explorer's path. Remember peaky Marco Polo? He wasn't a rock-hard mountaineer. He only climbed the perilous Pamirs to get from A to B. Mountains could also be horribly useful. Popocatepetl (a volcano in Mexico) was first climbed in the sixteenth century by Spanish soldiers looking for sulphur for making gunpowder*.

*Sulphur's found in the gases that volcanoes belch out. When it cools down, it forms crusty bright yellow crystals.

But it wasn't until the eighteenth century that people really began climbing mountains for the thrill of it. Before that, they just couldn't see the point.

Hardy Henriette

Today girls can do everything boys can do, like playing football or falling off a bike. But in the nineteenth century, things were different. Horribly different. Girls were expected to stay at home doing boring things like knitting and looking after the house. They certainly weren't expected to go clambering up slippery mountain slopes. Pity no one told that to daredevil Henriette d'Angeville.

Horrible Health Warning

If you're up a peak and you get the giggles, get down the mountain. FAST. You could be suffering from mountain sickness. And it's no laughing matter. It feels a bit like the flu with a splitting headache and a hacking cough. Bursting out laughing's another symptom. At best, you'll feel very peaky. At worst, you'll soon be dead. Mountain sickness is brought on by the lack of oxygen high up, though early climbers used to blame the demons they thought lived on the freaky peaks.

DID YOU GIGGLE?

Horrible Geography Travellers' Tales

HENRIETTE D'ANGEVILLE (1795-1871) NATIONALITY: FRENCH

Henriette didn't give two hoots about being ladylike. And she couldn't stand knitting. Nope. She'd set her sights much higher than that: on mighty Mont Blanc in the Alps. Henriette's dream was to become the first woman to climb this freaky peak, the highest in Europe at 4,807 metres tall. Her family tried their best to talk her out of it. They were worried about what people might think. But the more they nagged Henriette, the more determined she was to go.

Living the high life

Henriette spent months planning her expedition and on 2 September 1838 she set off. Good job her fretful family didn't know what she was wearing under her dress. A pair of brightly checked TROUSERS. They'd have been horrified. In those days, girls were expected to wear respectable, long, thick skirts.

Henriette hired some local guides to lead the way up the monstrous mountain. They reckoned she was incredibly brave (for a girl, that is). It took her three gruelling days to reach the top. She even had to spend one night in a cave without any food or blankets. From the summit, she sent off a carrier pigeon with news of her success. Then instead of a nice, warming cup of tea, she cracked open a bottle of ice-cold champagne and drank a high-rise toast.

WOULD YOU LIKE ICE?

ICE? I'D LIKE MINE BOILED!

Earth-shattering fact
Strictly speaking, Henriette wasn't the first woman to reach the top of Mont Blanc. A local girl, Maria Paradis, decided to make some money and set up a stall on the summit selling food to peckish climbers. She climbed as high as she could on her own, then had to be carried the rest of the way. At least hardy Henriette made it on her own two feet.

More high-flying heroines

Henriette's amazing adventure was brilliant news for girls and lots of intrepid women followed her daring lead. Why were they willing to brave the freezing cold and howling winds? Not to mention the risk of being swept downhill by an awful avalanche? It's a very good question. But anything was better than housework, and knitting…

Lucy Walker (1836–1916) came from a climbing family. Her father and brother were top mountaineers and Lucy had climbed loads of peaks with them. On 20 July 1871 intrepid Lucy became the first woman to climb the mighty Matterhorn in the Alps. She celebrated reaching the top with a nice glass of champagne and a slice of sponge cake.

Annie Smith Peck (1850–1935) was a dead-clever university professor. But in her spare time she headed for the hills. In 1908, she became the first person to climb lofty Mount Huascaran in the Andes in Peru. It was sixth time lucky for adventurous Annie who described the whole thing as "a horrible nightmare".

Fanny Bullock Workman (1859–1925) was bike mad. But in 1898 she pedalled off to the Himalayas in Asia and was bitten by the climbing bug. Her career reached a peak in 1906 when she climbed the 6,930-metre-high Pinnacle Peak, a world record for a woman. Then in 1912 she set off to scale the gruelling Siachen Glacier, the longest in Asia. Howling  winds almost blew her tent away and a guide fell down a crevasse. By mistake, news reached the papers at home that it was Fanny, not the guide, who'd died.

Elizabeth Burnaby (1861–1934) got into climbing on doctor's orders. The fresh air would do her good, he said. Ladylike Liz wore a long skirt for climbing but with trousers underneath. As soon as she was out of sight, she took the skirt off and hid it under a rock. In between getting married (three times), she climbed Mont Blanc twice and became president of the first ladies' climbing club.

Even though it was tough at the top, these plucky women were mountain mad. Despite all the ups and downs, they were crazy about climbing. But not every budding climber was quite so hooked on freaky peaks.

Moaning Manning

In 1811, eccentric British explorer Thomas Manning reached the mysterious city of Lhasa, high up in Tibet. Even though he travelled in disguise, it was a risky route to take. In those days, lofty Lhasa was closed to visitors. If Manning had been spotted he'd probably have been killed. Did Manning thank his lucky stars for making it in one piece? Did he heck? He was much too busy moaning.

Horrible Geography Travellers' Tales

Young Thomas was brilliant at lessons. He got top marks in Latin, Greek and maths and went to Cambridge University where he learned Chinese. What a clever-clogs. But Tom wasn't a ghastly goody-goody always sucking up to his teachers. He never took anything seriously and was always cracking corny jokes.

A slow boat to China

Manning was desperate to go to China to see the place for himself. Trouble is, foreigners were banned from China so he needed a good excuse to get in. Guess what he did? He went off to study medicine so he could work as a doctor.

(Doctors and scientists in general were highly respected in China.) He also wore long Chinese robes and grew a long beard. Manning reckoned the beard made him look rather dashing though none of his friends agreed.

At first, Manning tried to reach China by sea but his ship was turned back. So he decided to take a riskier and more roundabout route. He'd start off in India, head over the Himalayas into Tibet, then try to make his way from there into China. Brilliant, eh? There was just one small problem with Manning's foolproof plan. He wasn't at all intrepid. Not the teeniest little bit. OK, so he desperately wanted to go to China, but he absolutely hated travelling. And he never stopped moaning about it! Here's how mardy Manning might have described his journey in his letters home to a friend.

Summer 1811
Calcutta, India

My dear friend Charles,
I'm just leaving Calcutta in India. Goodness knows where I'll end up. Oh well. I reckon it's only another 5,000 kilometres to go until I reach China. Depressing, isn't it? I must say, Charles, this exploring lark isn't all it's cracked up to be. Why, oh why didn't I listen to you and stay at home? I'll try to write again soon (if I live that long, that is).
     Wish I was there,
     From Tom

P.S. The beard's coming along nicely, by the way. It's almost down to my knees.

Mid-November 1811
Gyantse, Tibet

Dear Charles,
Here I am in Tibet and things are going well. Who am I
kidding? What an awful journey! A few weeks after leaving
Calcutta, I reached Bhutan (a tiny Himalayan kingdom)
and the start of those murderous mountains. Grrr! Since
then, it's been uphill all the way.

No wonder I collapsed with exhaustion. (Thank goodness for
my recipe for stewed turnips - what a nourishing dish
when you're ill.) And my poor feet are killing me. The
weather's been terrible. It did nothing but rain for days
on end and I got wet through. I'm soooo miserable!
        Anyway, I finally reached Phari-dzong Fort just over
the border in Tibet. I was looking forward to a good rest but
a local big-wig turned up out of the blue and I got turfed
out of my nice, comfy bed. Typical.

The last leg of the journey to Gyantse was ghastly. My horse got spooked and bolted. Thank goodness a herd of yaks got in the way and stopped it in its tracks. Otherwise I'd be a goner. I WANNA GO HOME!

From Tom

P.S. I've had to stop sleeping in my clothes — they're full of flipping fleas! Hopping mad? I'm furious!

December 1811
Lhasa, Tibet

Dear Charles,
Lhasa at last! But more of that later. Getting here's been a nightmare. I've never been so cold in my life. Even in my new sheepskin coat and hat, it was so chilly that icicles grew on my beard. Crossing the mountains was murder. The paths were so icy that one false step and you'd plummet to your doom. If I ever make it back home, I never want to see a miserable mountain again. Not even a horrible hill.

As we approached Lhasa, I must confess I had high hopes of the place. I even cracked a few jokes, which I haven't done for ages. But my hopes were quickly dashed. What a grim, gloomy place this is! I'm so disappointed. And after I've come all this way. I'm sorry, Charles, I'm too depressed to write any more.

See you soon, I hope.
From Tom

Homeward bound

After all that, Manning never made it to China. His request was sent to the Chinese Emperor but it was turned down. Worse still, the city authorities guessed Manning was an impostor. Even though they couldn't prove it, his every move was watched. At least he was able to make his living as a doctor. Until a patient died, that is. Then he had to sell his spare clothes to make ends meet. At last, in April 1812, Manning was allowed to leave Lhasa and return to England. So what do you think he did next?

a) He wrote a book about his trip.
b) He wrote a book about beards.
c) He wrote a joke book.

Answer: c) Manning never bothered to write up the diary he kept on his Lhasa trip. In fact, no one knew it even existed until years after his death. Instead he wrote a brilliant book of corny jokes. Have you heard the one about the moaning minnie with the beard down to his knees?

MAYBE I SHOULD WRITE A BOOK ABOUT CORNY BEARDS.

Apart from a holiday in Italy, Manning never travelled again. But that didn't stop him moaning. And in case all his whingeing is starting to get you down, let's move swiftly on. Our next intrepid explorer couldn't wait to hit the road.

Brilliant Bingham

This is the story of a man on a mission. A mission to find a long-lost city and its secret stash of gold. The man was American explorer Hiram Bingham. Apart from being horribly brave, Hiram was also brilliant at climbing. He needed to be. The reason the city had been lost for so long was because it was perched high up on a freaky peak.

Horrible Geography Travellers' Tales

HIRAM BINGHAM
(1875-1956)
NATIONALITY:
AMERICAN

At university, brainy Hiram studied history and later became a professor. But in 1911 he was asked to lead an expedition to South America and he jumped at the chance. Well, what would you have done in his shoes? Set off on the adventure of a lifetime? Or stayed at home and become a boring history teacher?

Hiram's mission sounded simple. He had to find the ancient Inca city of Vilcampampa. Trouble was, mysterious Vilcampampa had been lost for centuries.

Earth-shattering fact
The Incas lived in the Andes around 700 years ago. For hundreds of years they had it all – a vast empire, beautiful cities, a flourishing religion and pots and pots of gold. Then disaster struck. In the sixteenth century, Spanish soldiers called conquistadors (that means

conquerors) arrived in Peru. They weren't bothered about cities or gods. They were greedy for Inca gold. Faced with Spanish guns, the Incas couldn't fight back and were brutally wiped out. Many Inca cities were ransacked but a few survived. They were so well hidden in the mountains, the Spanish hadn't a clue they were even there.

Legend had it that Vilcampampa was a secret mountain stronghold where the Incas had hidden from the Spanish. It had fabulous palaces, fine temples and treasure beyond your wildest dreams. So the story said. If anyone could track it down, hardy Hiram could. Here's how the *Daily Globe* might have reported the findings of Hiram's hair-raising trek.

25 July   *The Daily Globe*   1911

Cuzco, Peru

LOST INCA CITY FOUND IN ANDES

HERO HIRAM

Ace American explorer Hiram Bingham was back in Cuzco today celebrating a fabulous find. A daring expedition led by Bingham has just discovered a long-lost Inca city, high up in the awesome Andes mountains.

A beaming Bingham told our reporter, "I couldn't believe my eyes. I knew the city must be somewhere in the mountains but I hadn't the foggiest where." It was remarkable that Bingham found the ancient city at all. The only clue to its whereabouts came from an old Spanish manuscript. It said the city probably lay "…over beyond the ranges in the region where I had seen snow-capped peaks…" It wasn't a lot to go on but it was all Bingham had. He reckoned the city must be near Cuzco, in a part of the Andes never explored before. But it was only a guess.

Into the unknown

A few weeks ago, Bingham and his team set out from Cuzco on the first leg of their intrepid trek. They rode on mule-back along a steep-sided river valley with towering peaks on either side. The view was breathtaking.

"I know of no place in the world which can compare with it," Bingham told us. "Not only has it great snow peaks looming above the clouds more than two miles overhead, gigantic precipices of many-coloured granite rising sheer for thousands of feet above the foaming, glistening, roaring rapids; it also has, in striking contrast, orchids and tree ferns, the delectable beauty of luxurious vegetation, and the mysterious witchery of the jungle."

A stroke of luck

But there was still no sign of a city. Then Bingham had a sensational stroke of luck. A local farmer told him about some Inca ruins on a nearby peak. Could these be what Bingham had been looking for? He didn't have high hopes. But next morning he set off to find out once and for all. It was a long, gruelling climb up steep slopes covered in thick jungle creepers which were too green and slippery to grip.

SLIPPERY SLOPE

"At times, we had to crawl on all fours," he told our reporter, "sometimes clinging on by our fingertips. Below us were raging rapids. Above us were snow-capped peaks."

But was Bingham on the brink of a breathtaking discovery? Or would it turn out to be a wild-goose chase? He didn't have to wait long to find out. For just around the corner, an extraordinary sight met his eyes – the ruins of an ancient Inca city, lost for centuries.

A dream come true

For Bingham, it seemed like a dream. The long-abandoned buildings were overgrown with trees and moss, but he could make out the ruins of ancient houses and temples, crumbling walls and flights of steps. There was one surprise after another…

"Suddenly we found ourselves standing in front of the ruins of two of the finest and most interesting structures in ancient America," Bingham told us. "Made of beautiful white granite, the walls contained blocks of colossal size, higher than a man. The sight held me spellbound."

Bingham called the city Machu Picchu after the freaky peak it perched on. He was lucky to find it at all. From the river valley below, this city's completely hidden from view. Bingham told our reporter he'll be back next year for a more detailed dig. And judging by what he's unearthed so far, things should get very exciting.

Maybe he'll find the buried treasure said to lie under the city. Readers of the *Daily Globe* won't miss a thing. With our exclusive coverage, you'll be kept up to date with the latest thrilling developments.

THE CITY AT THE END OF THE RAINBOW

But were these high-rise ruins Vilcampampa? Bingham thought (wrongly) they were. In fact, he'd stumbled on a sacred Inca city built around 550 years ago. His amazing discovery put Machu Picchu well and truly on the map. Today, thousands of budding explorers follow in Bingham's footsteps and set off for Machu Picchu along the Inca trail every year. But be warned. If you're thinking of joining them, you'll need a good head for heights. The city's perched on the side of a freaky peak more than 2,500 metres high.

Meanwhile, on the other side of the world, crazy climbers had another peaky problem to crack. Forget long-lost cities and rambling ruins. Mount Everest, the highest peak on the planet at 8,848 metres, had yet to be climbed. The question was: who'd be the first person to stand on top of the world? Whoever it was would need to be as tough as old boots, brave and fighting fit. Luckily, the two men in the next story fitted the bill perfectly.

Tough Tenzing and Hardy Hillary

In May 1953 Tenzing Norgay and Edmund Hillary became the most famous climbers ever. After a truly treacherous journey, this plucky pair finally reached the summit of Mount Everest, on the border of Tibet and Nepal. No one had climbed this high before. No one knew if you even could.

> *Earth-shattering fact*
> *Mount Everest was named after Sir George Everest (1790–1866), the first person to measure the mountain. His nickname was "Never-rest" because he was such a slave-driver. Good job they didn't call the mountain that. The locals call this freaky peak Chomolungma (Mother Goddess of the World) or Sagarmatha (Goddess of the Sky).*

Horrible Geography Travellers' Tales

TENZING NORGAY
(1914 - 1986)
NATIONALITY:
NEPALESE

EDMUND HILLARY
(born 1919)
NATIONALITY:
NEW ZEALANDER

Hardy Edmund Hillary didn't get into climbing until he was 26 years old. He was too busy working in the family bee-keeping business to be buzzing off up freaky peaks. Tenzing, on the other hand, had climbing in his blood. Born and brought up in the Himalayas, he'd been scrambling up massive mountains since he was a lad. Both men had attempted to climb Everest before but had been forced back by freezing weather and gale-force winds before they'd reached the top. This time, they were determined to go one better. Even if it meant dicing with death.

Feeling intrepid? You'll need to be. If Tenzing and Hillary had kept a video diary of their record-breaking climb, here's how it might have gone…

A mountain to climb
Mount Everest, 29 May 1953

110

After breakfast, we started getting everything ready for the climb to the summit. We've checked and double-checked the oxygen tanks, ropes and ice axes. Without them, we won't survive. It's −27°C inside the tent and Hillary's leather boots have frozen solid. Here he is cooking them over the camping stove to thaw them out.

05:30   REC ☀

We left Camp Nine at 6.30 am and headed for the South Summit (a smaller peak before the main summit) up this long, steep snow slope. We've been taking it in turns to lead — it's Tenzing's turn now. Trouble is, the soft, deep snow lies over a thin icy crust which keeps shattering beneath our feet. It's like walking on meringues. For every five steps we climb, we slide back another three. So progress has been horribly slow.

08:00   REC ☀

111

We reached the South Summit at 9 am – so far, so good. Then it was off along the knife-sharp ridge leading to the summit proper. We had to watch our step, though – the sides of the ridge were sheer and slippery. Luckily, the snow was hard and firm and we cut steps into it with our ice axes. Even so, we roped ourselves together. Better safe than sorry.

09:30   REC•

But now we've got a much bigger problem – you can see it behind us. There's a massive step of rock across the ridge, blocking our path. It's so steep there's no way of climbing it. And if we can't climb it, our hopes of reaching the summit are well and truly scuppered.

09:31   REC•

Just when we thought we'd have to turn back, Hillary noticed a wafer-thin crack between the rock at the right of the step and the icy overhang next to it. Call us foolhardy, but we decided to take our chance. Hillary squeezed himself in and began to pull himself up. I can hardly watch. If the ice gives way, he'll plummet on to the glacier below. But he's very nearly done it. He's nearly at the top. Incredible. Hang on, that means it's my turn next!

10:00   REC☼

Well, we've finally made it! We were worn out and all the time our strength was failing, but we staggered on. Then just above us, we saw a small, snow-covered hump. It didn't look like much but it was the summit of Everest! The highest point on Earth. At last! So here we are admiring the view. And what a view it is – nothing but empty sky all around. And no one's ever seen it before. Amazing, isn't it? It's been a long, hard slog but it's been worth it. We're on top of the world!

11:30   REC☼

Tenzing and Hillary only spent 15 minutes on the summit. They were running short of oxygen and couldn't stay long. Then it was back down to Earth with a bump. Back home, they were treated like superstars. Fancy living the high life like Tenzing and Hillary? Try this quick quiz to see if you're cut out for climbing.

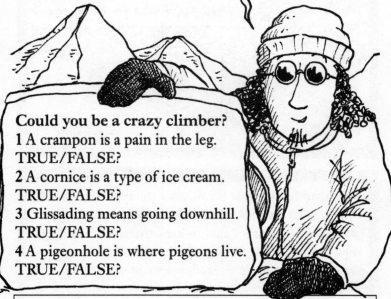

Could you be a crazy climber?
1 A crampon is a pain in the leg.
TRUE/FALSE?
2 A cornice is a type of ice cream.
TRUE/FALSE?
3 Glissading means going downhill.
TRUE/FALSE?
4 A pigeonhole is where pigeons live.
TRUE/FALSE?

Answers:
1 FALSE. That's cramp, silly. Crampons are sharp, pointy metal spikes you strap on to the soles of your climbing boots. Very handy for walking over icy ground without losing your grip.
2 FALSE. True, it's a type of ice but not the sort you scoff. A cornice is a colossal overhanging chunk of ice formed when howling winds blow along a mountain ridge. The ice can break loose at any time, causing climbers to come a cropper.

3 TRUE. Glissading is French for sliding. It means sliding down an icy slope on your feet or bum. If you find you're going downhill fast, try using your ice axe as a brake. In 1986, two crazy climbers glissaded 2,500 metres down Mount Everest. ON THEIR BOTTOMS! Bet they couldn't sit down for weeks.

WHO PUT THAT TREE THERE?!

4 FALSE. This pigeonhole's a type of step. And nothing to do with batty birds. But it's not the type of step you find on your staircase at home, covered in cosy carpet. Climbers use their ice axes to hack these slippery steps out of the ice. They're especially useful on steep, icy slopes where you need to clamber up on all fours.

So how did you do?

Award yourself ten peaky points for each correct answer.

40 points. Congratulations! You're at the peak of your powers and you'll make a top climber.

20–30 points. Not bad! You haven't reached the dizzy heights but you'll soon get to know the ropes.

10 points and below. Forget it! Climbing's not for you. You'd better keep your feet firmly on the ground.

Earth-shattering fact
Since Tenzing and Hillary's time, hundreds of crazy climbers have reached the top of Everest. But despite all the posh gear and mod cons, it's still a horribly risky thing to do. Even for the experts. The weather can change at any minute ... often for the worse. In May 1996, top New Zealand climber Rob Hall found himself trapped by a blizzard just 150 metres short of the summit. Badly frostbitten, he had no tent, sleeping bag, water or food. Hall managed to call his wife on the radio telephone and told her not to worry and that he'd see her soon. But tragically he didn't make it and died soon afterwards.

Had enough of life at the top as a rock-hard mountaineer? Perhaps you'd prefer the perils of a perishing polar pioneer? Someone who'll go to the ends of the Earth in search of a really cool adventure? Come on, there's only one way to find out. Let's head for the parky Poles...

PØLAR PIØNEERS

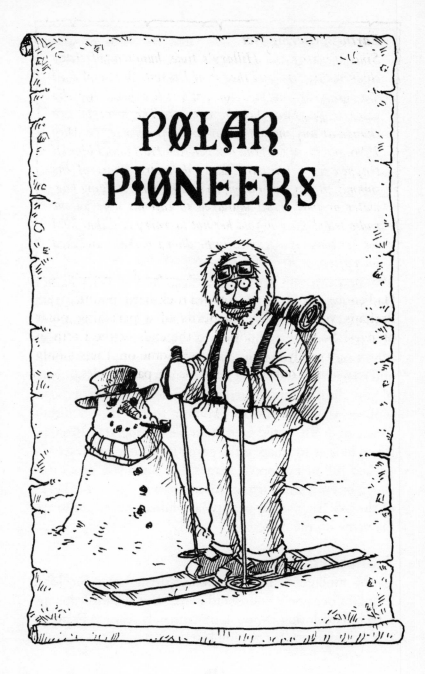

Imagine a place that's colder than the inside of your freezer. A place so teeth-chatteringly chilly that your breath freezes solid in front of your face and your hair turns to icicles. Welcome to the p-p-perishing Poles.

The first intrepid explorers to head for the Poles hadn't the foggiest what on Earth they were in for. But that didn't stop them going. Oh no. Some set off in search of new trade routes. Some hunted seals and whales. Others didn't care about making money, they wanted excitement and adventure (and they got it in bucketloads). Mind you, if you didn't mind d-icing with death, being a polar pioneer was the kind of explorer to be. If you didn't freeze to death, you'd be treated like a superstar. Besides, if you look at any map of the perishing Poles, you'll see it's packed full of explorers' names. Having a sea, or an ice-sheet, or even a seal named after you was one of the perks of the job. Shame our next polar pioneer never got to see his name on the map.

Fearless Franklin

In the nineteenth century, bold British sailor Sir John Franklin became a household name. But it wasn't for his intrepid exploring. Nope. Unfortunately fearless Franklin was dead famous for getting lost.

For centuries, intrepid explorers from Europe had been searching for a new trade route to the east. Trouble is, the way they picked lay right across the frozen far north of North America and through the iceberg-infested Arctic Ocean. It was called the North-West Passage and it was proving horribly hard to find.

Earth-shattering fact
British explorer Sir Martin Frobisher (1535–1594) didn't suffer fools gladly. He was tough, brave and rugged – all the things an explorer should be. In 1576, feisty Frobisher set sail in search of the North-West Passage. He didn't find it, but on icy Baffin Island he spotted a sparkling lump of rock. Frobisher was sure it was gold. Over the next two years, he made two more voyages and collected tonnes of the stuff. He was going to be filthy rich. Yippee! It must be worth a fortune. Or was it? Unfortunately for Frobisher, it turned out not to be gold at all, just worthless iron pyrite (that's a mixture of iron and sulphur). Some people call it "fool's gold". It certainly fooled poor old Frobisher.

Horrible Geography Travellers' Tales

SIR JOHN FRANKLIN (1786-1847) NATIONALITY: BRITISH

At the tender young age of 14, John left home and ran away to sea. He sailed to Australia, the Arctic (three times) and North America. You name it, he went there. By the time Franklin was 59 years old, he was looking forward to a well-earned rest. Instead he was picked to lead a daring new expedition to find the North-West Passage. Despite his age, Franklin was perfect for the job. He was brave and kind, and got on brilliantly with everyone. Besides, he was used to being in the thick of danger. And frankly, it was just as well.

Earth-shattering fact
In the Arctic, things aren't always what they seem (as foolish Frobisher found out). In 1818, British sailor John Ross (1777–1856) became the latest explorer to try to find the fabled Passage. And the latest to fail miserably. He did discover a range of mountains which he named the Croker Mountains after a Royal Navy admiral. But when another expedition tried to find them the following year, the mysterious mountains were nowhere to be seen. Ross had been seeing things. For the rest of his life, his nickname was, guess what? Yep, "Croker Mountains". Cruel!

Franklin sets off
In May 1845 Franklin set sail from England with two sturdy ships, *Erebus* and *Terror*, and a 130-man crew. The ships were fitted with all the latest mod cons. They even had central heating to keep the crew toasty warm. And they had a ship's monkey instead of a ship's cat. Franklin's plan was to head north to Greenland, then west across the north of North America through a murderous maze of icy islands and channels.

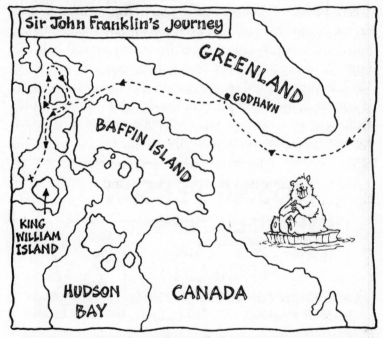

By July, Franklin had reached Greenland and wrote a cheery letter home. So far, so good. Two weeks later, a whaling ship spotted the ships moored to an iceberg to stop them drifting off. The curious captain went on board and had dinner with jolly Sir John. But I'm afraid this tale has a horribly sad ending. For fearless Franklin was never seen again...

The search for Franklin

Back home, no news was good news. At first. But as the years passed and there was still no word from Franklin, his friends began to fear the worst. Search party after search party was sent out and the rescuers tried everything to contact the missing men, including catching a load of foxes and tying notes to their collars. Bet that would have foxed Franklin. But it didn't do any good. Missing Franklin's whereabouts were still a mystery.

Meanwhile, Franklin's wife, Lady Jane, refused to give up her hubbie for lost. She even consulted a fortune teller, but there was no sign of Franklin in her crystal ball. So Lady Jane organized her own search party. It set off in 1857, led by salty old sea dog Captain Francis McClintock. If anyone could find Franklin, the doughty captain could. Especially as Lady Jane was offering a reward of £20,000 for news – a small fortune for the time…

MISSING PERSON

HAVE YOU SEEN THIS MAN?

NAME: SIR JOHN FRANKLIN

LAST KNOWN SIGHTING: July 1845, BAFFIN ISLAND, ARCTIC OCEAN.

★★★ **£20,000 REWARD** ★★★★

FOR NEWS OF SIR JOHN, HIS SHIPS OR CREWS.

APPLY TO: Lady Jane Franklin (c/o The Admiralty, London).

NOTE: PROOF WILL BE REQUIRED.

The search lasted for over a year, but in February 1859, Lady Jane got the news she'd been dreading. The search party had found a message written 12 years before by two of Franklin's most trusted men. It was buried under a pile of stones on King William Island. And it gave vital clues about Franklin's tragic fate. It started off like this…

H.M.S. Erebus and H.M.S. Terror
1847-1848
Whoever finds this paper is requested to forward it to the Secretary of the Admiralty, London, with a note of the time and place at which it was found. Or, if more convenient, to deliver it for that purpose to the British Consul at the nearest Port…

The note went on… In summer 1846, the ships were making steady progress and had the Passage in their sights. Then it all went horribly wrong. How? Well, Franklin took a wrong turning. Simple as that. It wasn't really Franklin's fault – the maps he was using got muddled. But it meant the ships sailed straight into the worst of the pack ice.* By September, they were stuck fast off King William Island. Franklin died the following June. Ten months later, the rest of the crew abandoned ship. Starving and scurvy-ridden, they headed south, hoping to reach the mainland. Sadly, they never made it. One by one, they died. Next to their skeletons the search party found the gruesome leftovers of their last meal. It seemed that when the men's meagre rations ran out, they'd been forced to eat … each other.

* Pack ice isn't anything to do with suitcases and going on your hols. Horrible geographers will tell you that in winter the Arctic Ocean freezes solid. Pack ice is broken bits of sea ice that drift on the wind and ocean currents. It's horribly hazardous to ships, as poor old Franklin found out.

Earth-shattering fact
The first person to sail through the North-West Passage was ace Norwegian explorer Roald Amundsen in 1906, thanks to his trusty boat, the Gjoa, which was small and nifty for nipping in and out of ice floes. Even then it took him three years. Guess who Amundsen dedicated his success to? None other than good old Franklin, his boyhood hero. (By the way, Amundsen became one of the greatest explorers EVER. Catch up with him again on page 132.)

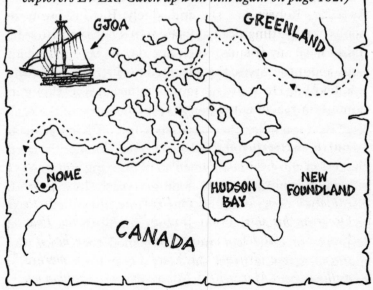

But finding the North-West Passage was only the tip of the iceberg. There was still the perishing North Pole to be conquered. And that's just where we're off to now…

Plucky Peary

This is the story of two men who both claimed to have reached the North Pole. The question is: which one of them got there first? Read on and see what you think.

Horrible Geography Travellers' Tales

ROBERT E PEARY
(1856-1920)
NATIONALITY:
AMERICAN

As a lad, Robert was shy and lonely. But his favourite hobby was stuffing dead animals so it's not surprising he didn't have any friends. Then one day he read a brilliant book about the Arctic that changed his life. Young Robert was hooked. He was determined to become an explorer, famous for reaching the North Pole first.

Earth-shattering fact
Norwegian Fridtjof Nansen (1861–1930) knew all about the awful Arctic. One of the greatest polar explorers ever, he set off in 1893 to cross the Arctic Ocean in his ship, Fram, *and drift towards the Pole. Fram's special design meant it wouldn't be crushed if it stuck in the drifting pack ice. The plan worked brilliantly. In March 1895 Nansen and a companion left*

125

the ship to ski to the North Pole. They went further north than anyone else but had to stop short of the Pole. Then things went from bad to worse. They were forced to spend a freezing winter in the Arctic, living on stewed polar bear. It wasn't until the following June that gutsy Nansen was finally rescued.

Peary joined the US Navy but luckily his bosses gave him plenty of time off for exploring. He made nine trips to the Arctic in all, pushing further and further north. Twice he tried to reach the North Pole but freezing weather forced him back. Parky Peary nearly starved to death and he lost half of his toes from frostbite. His toes simply snapped off when he took off his socks! How horrible is that?

But Peary was as hard as nails and he wasn't about to give up. No way. Toes or no toes, he was going to put his best foot forward.

In July 1908 Peary set off again for the Arctic. This would be his last chance to reach the North Pole. Would it be third time lucky for plucky Peary?

Earth-shattering fact
The local Arctic people are called the Inuit (Ee-noo-eet).
They've lived there for centuries and are experts at
coping with the perishing polar cold. Peary reckoned
(rightly) his best chance of survival was to live like a
local. So he made friends with some Inuit and picked up
loads of top survival tips. Like learning to drive a dog
sledge, build an igloo and make cosy clothes from seal and
polar bear skins. Think you could do any of these?

Third time lucky?

Early in 1909, Peary and his party set up camp on icy
Ellesmere Island, off Greenland. For months they busied
themselves laying supplies on the route to the Pole. Then
Peary set off. The journey was perilous. The fragile ice
beneath his feet threatened to crack at any time, plunging
his sledges into the freezing sea. And once he had to wait
six days for a stretch of water to freeze over.

127

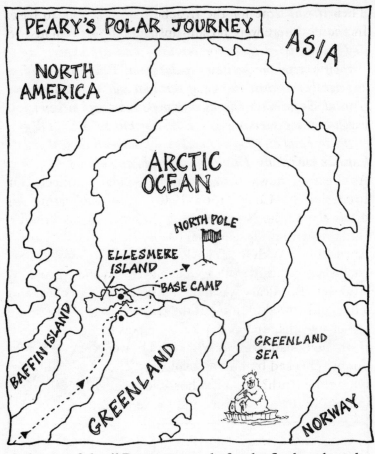

At last, on 2 April Peary was ready for the final push to the Pole. With him were four Inuit and his trusty travelling companion, Matthew Henson. For another five gruelling days, the men marched grimly on. Luckily, they made good progress. The ice was hard and level, and the sledges slid smoothly along. Then on 6 April 1909 came the moment Peary had been waiting for for so long. Utterly exhausted, he reached the North Pole at last. Peary and his companions planted an American flag and posed for photos.

Then it was time for the treacherous trek back to base. Incredibly, there were no slip-ups and it took them just 18 days.

So it seemed plucky Peary had reached the North Pole first and earned his place in history. Or had he? While Peary was patting himself on the back, another intrepid American explorer was celebrating EXACTLY THE SAME THING.

Cook's claim

As Peary's news broke, another polar pioneer, Dr Frederick A. Cook (1865–1940), was celebrating *his* discovery of the North Pole at a dinner in his honour. Bursting with pride, Cook said *he'd* reached the Pole on 21 April 1908, a WHOLE YEAR before Peary. Cook kept his cool when he heard of Peary's achievement and wished his rival well. But Peary was livid. He called Cook a cheat and a liar, and vowed to find out the truth.

For months, the polar punch-up was front-page news. Both men had kept diaries which were checked and double-checked by the top explorers' clubs. But who was telling the truth? Even the horrible geographers brought in to solve the matter once and for all couldn't agree...

Cook couldn't have got there first. Ask the Inuit who went with him. They said he stopped miles short of the Pole and swore them to secrecy. Oh, and that his North Pole piccies weren't of the Pole at all but somewhere else entirely.

Hmm. Puzzling, isn't it? So just who were you supposed to believe? Then a sensational story appeared in the newspapers...

October **The Daily Globe** 1909

New York, USA

CHEATING COOK IN McKINLEY SWINDLE

CROOKED COOK

The world of exploration was rocked last night by a sensational revelation. Dr Frederick A. Cook, celebrated conqueror of the North Pole, has been found guilty of cheating.

Three years ago we reported how Dr Cook led the first expedition to climb mighty Mount McKinley in Alaska, North America's highest peak. Overnight, his amazing trek turned him into a hero. But the *Daily Globe* can now reveal that Cook's fantastic feat was a fake.

According to Edward Barrill, Cook's companion on that ill-fated trip, they never reached the top at all. In fact, the photos of the summit were actually taken on another peak. What's more, their diaries were, er, doctored, on Cook's orders.

Today, Dr Cook wasn't available for interviews. Rumour has it he's already left New York in disguise and is lying low in Europe. But rival explorer Commander Robert E. Peary told our reporter, "Well, that proves it. There's no way he could have reached the North Pole either. He's been lying about it all along."

With his reputation in tatters, crestfallen Cook spent the rest of his life in disgrace. And the geographers ruled in Peary's favour, even though there wasn't any real proof to back up his claim. So the matter was settled. Or so it seemed. Some people still reckoned Peary was fibbing and hadn't been to the North Pole at all.

Earth-shattering fact
If you think Peary's claim was a lot of hot air, get this. In 1926, Italian Umberto Nobile (1885–1978) flew over the North Pole in an airship (like a giant hot-air balloon). His crew included famous co-pilot Roald Amundsen and Nobile's pet dog, Titina. This pampered pooch later became the first dog to see the North Pole twice. The trip was a huge success and Nobile was puffed up with pride. But on his next trip, two years later, tragedy struck when the airship crashed on to the ice. Nobile survived and was rescued but 17 lives were lost.

WHAT'S THE WEATHER LIKE?

RUFF!

Meanwhile, at the other end of the Earth the race for the South Pole was just about to start…

Awesome Amundsen

There is no doubt that Roald Amundsen was one of the world's greatest explorers. So why, when he set out on his most daring trip, did he decide not to tell anyone where on Earth he was going?

Horrible Geography Travellers' Tales

ROALD AMUNDSEN (1872-1928) NATIONALITY: NORWEGIAN

When Roald was 15 years old, he read a gripping book by Franklin and was bitten by the polar bug. Secretly he started toughening himself up for his first treacherous trip. In winter, he slept with his bedroom windows wide open. (He told his mum he found the fresh air bracing. Brrr.) And he was sickeningly fit and sporty from playing footie and skiing.

Roald trained to be a doctor but gave it up to be an explorer. He signed on as a sailor on a ship bound for Antarctica. Unfortunately, the ship got stuck in the ice and Roald had to spend the winter there. But even that didn't put him off. Soon he was planning his most daring trip yet – to reach the perishing North Pole. Everything was ready. Or so he thought. Then he received the earth-shattering news – Peary had got there first! What do you think Amundsen did instead?

a) He went to the North Pole anyway?
b) He gave it all up as a bad job and stayed at home?
c) He secretly set sail for the South Pole?

Answer: c) Ambitious Amundsen immediately put his North Pole plans on ice. But he didn't tell anyone yet. On 7 June 1910, he set sail from Norway in his sturdy ship, *Fram*, which he'd borrowed from Nansen (remember him?) and headed ... south instead of north. Only then did he tell his confused crew. He said they could leave on full pay if they wished but not one of them jumped ship.

Southward bound

Not everyone took the news so well. Dashing British explorer Captain Robert Falcon Scott (1869–1912) was already sailing south on *his* way to the Pole. The first thing he knew about Amundsen's change of plan was a troubling telegram...

Beg leave to inform you. *Fram* proceeding Antarctic...

You can imagine how miffed Scott must have felt. But there was no turning back now – the race for the Pole was on.

Six months after leaving Norway, *Fram* landed at the Bay of Whales on the Ross Ice Shelf (an enormous floating sheet of ice about the same size as France). Amundsen and his party set up their camp, called Framheim after their trusty ship, and settled in for the long, cold winter. OK, so a freezing cold lump of ice might not sound like the sort of campsite you'd pick, but clued-up Amundsen knew exactly what he was doing. He was 100 kilometres closer to the South Pole than Scott, and he hadn't even set off yet! Clever, eh?

There was plenty for the men to do while they waited for spring to come. They kept busy laying stores on their route to the Pole, braving bone-chilling temperatures of -50°C.

At last on 20 October, the waiting was finally over. With four men, 52 dogs and four sledges loaded with supplies, Amundsen struck out for the Pole. Did he beat Scott to it? Did he make it back alive? Where better to look for the answers than in Amundsen's own expedition diary? Don't worry, we've translated it specially for you from Norwegian. (Amundsen's actual diary went almost like this but not quite.)

Earth-shattering fact
Before you get stuck in, here's a quick word about dogs. Yep, dogs. But not ordinary pet pooches who chew slippers and dig up your dad's best plants. No, these top dogs were hardy huskies from Greenland. Dogged Amundsen knew the fastest way to cross the ice was by dog sledge. So he let huskies do all the hard work. They were tough, well-trained and super-strong. A team of ten huskies could pull a sledge 50 kilometres a day, dragging the men along behind on skis. So there was no reason to get dog-tired!

TOP DOG!

134

MY OFFICIAL SOUTH POLE DIARY
by Roald Amundsen

22 October 1911, Ross Ice Shelf
Two days out and the weather's been wretched. We couldn't see a thing in the driving snow and one of the sledges fell down a crevasse. Thankfully, we managed to haul it back up, along with our precious supplies. If we'd lost those, we'd have been scuppered. We haven't brought along any spares.

17 November 1911, Transantarctic Mountains
Yippee! We've reached the halfway mark and I'm glad to say we're making better progress. The weather's been fine, the going's been good and the dogs have been brilliant. If we carry on like this, we'll be there in no time at all. And we'll definitely beat that slow-coach Scott. So fingers crossed.

20 November 1911, Axel Heiberg Glacier
Who was I kidding? Talk about famous last
words. It's taken us four back-breaking
days to climb this gruesome glacier. Goodness
knows how we made it. Talk about a slippery
slope. It was riddled with hidden crevasses
and giant rocks and blocks of ice. Terrifying.
Still, the good news is we've reached the
polar plateau*. Not far
to go now.

*That's a vast, flat
expanse of ice around
the South Pole.

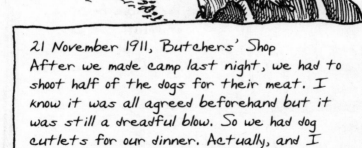

21 November 1911, Butchers' Shop
After we made camp last night, we had to
shoot half of the dogs for their meat. I
know it was all agreed beforehand but it
was still a dreadful blow. So we had dog
cutlets for our dinner. Actually, and I
hate to say it, they tasted delicious.

Yes, I know it sounds cruel and heartless. Especially if your pet pooch is curled up next to you on the sofa. But I'm afraid it's a dog-eat-dog world at the Poles. Amundsen didn't have time to be soppy or he'd have starved to death. Besides, fresh dog meat was brilliant for warding off scurvy (remember that deadly disease?). Sorry.

WHAT?

26 November 1911, Polar Plateau
What a nightmare! Just as we were moving off, the weather broke. And how! Howling winds and blinding blizzards swept across the plateau. And for four days we were holed up in the tent. In the end we decided to make a dash for it. We've still got the dicey Devil's Glacier to climb. I only hope it doesn't live up to its name.

137

8 December 1911, Polar Plateau (still)
Crossing the glacier took three gruelling days.
It was worse than I thought. The dogs kept
falling through the ice, followed by the men,
and we spent hours pulling them out again.

But things are looking up now. The weather's
changed completely and guess what? We've
got brilliant sunshine and blue skies.
Nothing could spoil our happy mood. Well, almost
nothing. One of the men thought he'd spotted
Scott up ahead. But luckily it turned out
he was seeing things.

14 December 1911, the South Pole
We've made it. We've finally made it. I
can't believe I'm really here. The South
Pole! None of us felt like speaking. We
didn't know what to say. So we shook hands
instead. Then we planted the Norwegian flag
in the snow and posed for some photos.

There's no sign of Scott but we've left him a note and some supplies. Right, now I'm off to take some readings to prove we're really here.

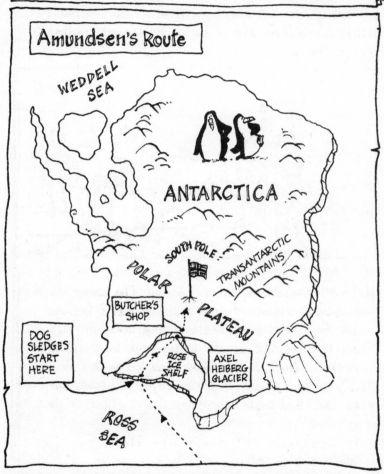

Amundsen spent three days at the South Pole, then he and his men set off on the long journey back to base. Six weeks later, they reached Framheim, safe and fighting fit. Amazingly, they'd completed their historic 2,500-kilometre trip in just over three months. An awesome achievement.

139

Scott comes second

But where on Earth was Captain Scott? As Amundsen posed for piccies at the Pole, Scott was in deep trouble 640 kilometres away. One problem was, while Amundsen's hardy huskies sped across the ice, Scott's men pulled their sledges themselves.

Why? Well, Scott thought it was a more manly thing to do. But it was back-breaking work and quickly took its terrible toll on Scott's men.

Despite the desperately slow going, on 17 January 1912 Scott and his four hardy companions – Edgar Evans, Lawrence Oates, Birdie Bowers and Edward Wilson – finally made it to the South Pole, only to find that their worst fears had come true. Amundsen had beaten them to it by more than a month.

Nightmare journey

With their spirits broken, Scott and his men began their journey home. Suffering from scurvy and frostbite, their strength quickly began to fail. Evans died on 17 February after falling into a crevasse. Oates's feet were so badly frostbitten he did not think he could carry on. Rather than hold the others back, he walked out into a blizzard and was never seen again. By mid–March, food and fuel were running desperately low. What's more, the weather took a turn for the worse with howling winds and driving snow. The three survivors, Scott, Wilson and Bowers, found themselves trapped in their tent, waiting for the weather to clear. But, weakened by hunger and illness, at the end of April they too died. Their tent and frozen bodies were found the following November by a rescue party. Little did the doomed men know that they were just 18 kilometres away from a supply depot stocked with food and fuel that would have saved their lives.

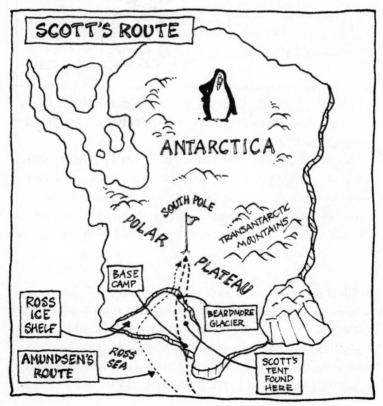

Earth-shattering fact
Another member of Scott's party, Apsley Cherry-Garrard (1886–1959) wasn't picked for the final push on the Pole. But he had had enough adventure to last him a lifetime. The previous winter (remember in Antarctica the seasons are the other way round? So it's winter in June and July), "Cherry", Wilson and Bowers had already made their own epic journey ... to collect a penguin egg! It was pitch black and the temperature fell below -70°C. But it wasn't just teeth-chatteringly cold. No. It was so perishing their teeth shattered and fell out. Almost dead on their feet, they pulled their sledges 90 kilometres to the penguin rookery at Cape Crozier, and 90 kilometres back. They suffered appallingly. When they reached the rookery, they were pinned down by a vicious storm.

Their tent blew away and for two days they lay shivering in their sleeping bags, singing hymns and waiting to die. Finally, the wind died down and they began the long slog back to base. Against all the odds, they staggered home, safe and sound, clutching their precious eggs. Cherry was lucky to be alive. Here's what he said:

> Polar exploration is at once the cleanest and most isolated way of having a bad time that has ever been devised...
>
> *Cherry later wrote a best-selling book about his treacherous trip. Its terrible title summed up how unspeakably gruelling it had been. He called it* The Worst Journey in the World.

For sheer guts and determination, Scott's ill-fated expedition would be horribly hard to beat. Even for a real tough nut like our next intrepid explorer. Luckily, he survived his perilous polar ordeal without cracking up under the strain ... but it was a very close shave.

Shivering Shackleton

Explorer Ernest Shackleton didn't believe in leaving anything to chance. When he wanted a crew for his latest perilous polar journey, he simply put an ad in the newspaper.

Men wanted for hazardous journey
Small wages, bitter cold.
Long months of complete darkness.
Constant danger, safe return doubtful.
Honour and recognition in case
of success.

NEW! FLUFFY-DUCK SLIPPERS ⟹

Incredibly, 5,000 men applied. Then Shackleton picked the 28 pluckiest.

Horrible Geography Travellers' Tales

SIR ERNEST
SHACKLETON
(1874-1922)
NATIONALITY:
IRISH

Young Ernest was often in trouble at school. His teachers said he spent too much time daydreaming. And it was true. In Ernest's dreams he wasn't stuck in a boring lesson. He was a top polar explorer. And guess what? Yep, his dream came true. When Ernest was 16, he ran away to sea. He almost reached the South Pole twice (once with Captain Scott) but was beaten back by woeful weather. Now enterprising Ernest had a new and daring plan. He wanted to cross the icy Antarctic continent from the Weddell Sea to the Ross Sea, via the South Pole. Shackleton spent months frantically raising funds and preparing for his trip. Then on 8 August 1914, the Boss* and his hand-picked crew set sail from England on board the *Endurance*, Shackleton's sturdy ship

*That was Shackleton's nickname. But he wasn't a bossy boots. Shackleton was a born leader. But he never got his men to do anything he wouldn't do himself. So they followed him through thick and thin.

Sounds exciting, doesn't it? But would you have volunteered? Shackleton's plan was to land at Vahsel Bay on the Weddell Sea, then to make the crossing in 100 days using dog sledges. Another ship would be waiting to pick them up at McMurdo Sound on the Ross Sea.

SHACKLETON'S (PROPOSED) ROUTE:

WEDDELL SEA

HALLEY BAY

ANTARCTICA

RONNE ICE SHELF

ANTARCTIC PENINSULA

PENSACOLA MOUNTAINS

SOUTH POLE

POLAR PLATEAU

ROSS ICE SHELF

McMURDO SOUND

ROSS SEA

Ahead of them lay a polar trek so dangerous no one had ever tried it before. Fortunately, Shackleton and his courageous crew were made of stern stuff. Which was just as well. You see, right from the start their daring trip didn't exactly go according to plan...

145

Icebound in Antarctica

Polar Progress Report 01

Date: January 1915

O *Location: Weddell Sea, Antarctica*

Progress so far: After leaving its last port of call on the island of South

O Georgia, the *Endurance* heads south into the ice-infested water of the Weddell Sea. At first, the *Endurance* rams a clear passage through the ice. Then disaster strikes. On 19 January, the pack ice is so thick that the *Endurance* sticks fast. The whole sea freezes around her and soon she's frozen solid, like

the stick in a lollipop. The men try to smash open a channel with picks and shovels. But it makes no difference. Worse still, their destination at Vahsel Bay is just one day's sail away.

Earth-shattering fact

The Weddell Sea was named after English sea captain James Weddell (1787–1834), who set off to Antarctica in 1822 in search of seals to hunt. Fortunately for Weddell, the weather that year was amazingly mild and clear. In fact Weddell wrote that "not a particle of ice of any description was to be seen..." Bet Shackleton wished he'd had half of Weddell's luck.

Polar Progress Report 02
Date: October 1915
O *Location: Weddell Sea*
Progress so far: For months
the drifting ice drags the
Endurance further and
further from land. The men

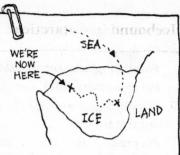

are forced to spend winter on board the trapped ship.
O They can't even tell anyone where they are - the
ship's radio doesn't work. When spring comes, they
hope to find a clear channel through the ice floes.
But spring's a very long way off. Shackleton tries to
keep the men's spirits up. They play football on the
ice and put on plays to pass the time but boredom
quickly sets in. And every day the ice tightens its
O grip on the ship. Soon she begins to crack up and
springs leak after leak. On 27 October, Shackleton
reluctantly gives the order to abandon ship.

Polar Progress Report 03
O *Date: November 1915*
Location: Weddell Sea
Progress so far: The men
salvage what they can from
the ship and pack it on to
O the sledges. They also haul
down the three lifeboats.

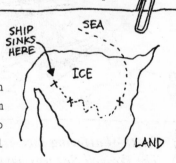

They then set up camp on the ice. Shackleton's dreams
of crossing the continent are well and truly
shattered. He tells the disappointed men that
they'll try to head for home. Then on 21 November,
O they watch in horror as the *Endurance* finally breaks
up and sinks beneath the ice.

Polar Progress Report 04
Date: April 1916
Location: Elephant Island

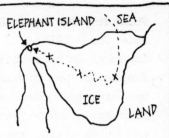

Progress so far: For the past six months, Shackleton and his men have been drifting on a raft of ice. They hope that the ice will carry them within reach of land, hundreds of kilometres away. But their hopes are soon dashed. The ice starts to crack up and their camp's no longer safe. On 9 April Shackleton orders the lifeboats to be launched in a desperate attempt to reach land.

Despite badly frostbitten hands, the men take turns to row. At night they camp on an ice floe but it's horribly dicey. One night the ice splits open and a man plunges into the perishing sea in his sleeping bag. Luckily, Shackleton manages to pull him out again. Seconds later, the ice closes over again. After that, they sleep in the boats. Six days later, they reach isolated Elephant Island. It's a year and a half since they last set foot on solid ground. Exhausted and hungry, many of the men are at breaking point.

Polar Progress Report 05
Date: April 1916
Location: Southern Ocean
Progress so far: No sealers or whalers come near Elephant Island so there's no hope of rescue.

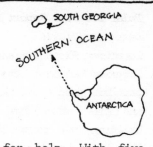

Shackleton decides to go for help. With five volunteers, he sets out in the *James Caird*, one of the lifeboats. His daring plan is to head to the whaling station on South Georgia from where they set out so long ago. Trouble is, to get there he has to cross some 1,200 kilometres of the Southern Ocean, the world's most dangerous sea. But there's nothing else for it - without help, the men left behind on Elephant Island won't last long. The journey's a nightmare. Giant waves and gale-force winds threaten to capsize the small boat.

Thick ice cakes the deck and has to be chipped off before the weight of it sinks the boat. The men are frozen and soaking wet. And their sleeping bags ice over so there's nowhere warm to rest. Besides, finding a tiny island in the middle of a vast ocean is like finding a needle in a haystack.

Polar Progress Report 06
Date: May 1916
Location: South Georgia
Progress so far: After 14 dreadful days at sea, the men finally sight land. Just in time. Two of them are very close to death. But the sea's much too choppy to land safely. Vicious winds drive them towards the cliffs where the little boat will surely be smashed to smithereens on the jagged rocks. This must be the end of the road.

Then, three days later, on 10 May, they somehow manage to steer into a small, sheltered bay. Now for a good, long rest. But their awful ordeal's not over yet. Unfortunately, the whaling station lies ... on the other side of the island!

Polar Progress Report 07
Date: May 1916
Location: Stromness Bay, South Georgia
Progress so far: On the afternoon of 20 May, three men stumble into Stromness Bay on South Georgia.

They're filthy, wild-eyed and dressed in rags, and the first people they meet run away. For the past 36 appalling hours, they've slogged non-stop over lethal, glacier-covered peaks to reach the whaling station. It's a miracle they've made it alive. Especially as their only equipment was one measly rope, an ice axe, a camping stove and three days'

food rations stuffed into their socks. They've had no maps to guide them. No one has ever crossed the island before. But at least they're finally safe.

Polar Progress Report 08
Date: August 1916
Location: Elephant Island
Progress so far: After three false starts, Shackleton sails back to Elephant Island to rescue his stranded men. Since he

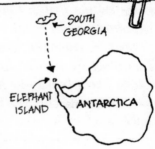

last saw them, they've suffered horribly. They've been forced to spend the winter living under their upturned boats and eating seal bones and seaweed stew. And they've almost given up hope of being saved. When they spot Shackleton's ship, they can't believe their eyes.

So shivering Shackleton's extraordinary story has a happy ending. Amazingly, he and his intrepid men survived against all the odds. Not a single life was lost in the greatest tale of polar exploration ever.

Earth-shattering fact
Sadly for Shackleton, his dreams of crossing the Antarctic continent were well and truly dashed. But daring British explorer Sir Vivian Fuchs (1908–1999) succeeded where Shackleton had failed. In 1957–58, Fuchs led the British Commonwealth Trans-Antarctic Expedition which made the first overland crossing of Antarctica from the Weddell Sea to the Ross Sea. Travelling by sno-cat (a tractor that runs on metal tracks, like a tank) and dog sledge, Fuchs and his 12-man party made the gruelling 3,500-kilometre journey in 99 days.

DID YOU BRING THE ROAD MAP?

Could you be a polar pioneer?
If someone gave you pemmican what would you do with it?
a) Eat it?
b) Wear it?
c) Feed it to the dog?

Answer: Both **a)** and **c)** are right. Pemmican's a nourishing food which polar explorers (and their pooches) used to scoff. It was crammed full of energy to keep them warm. Feeling peckish? Fancy rustling up some pemmican for tea? Here's the revolting recipe...

PEMMICAN PIE RECIPE

Ingredients:
☆ dried meat (beef or horse)
☆ fat or lard
☆ crushed biscuits
☆ onions or other veg (optional)
☆ curry powder (optional)

What to do:
1. Mix all the ingredients together.
2. Pack into a box or tin.

Note: That's all there is to it. Easy, isn't it?
You don't need to cook it and it'll last for years and years. So it's brilliant for long sledging trips.
And you thought school dinners were disgusting!

So, you've seen enough ice to last a lifetime. And you're looking forward to a change of scene? Somewhere nice and peaceful where you can drift along gently and watch the world go by? Well, you're in luck. Hurry up and hop on board. There are still a few places left on Miles' relaxing river tour.

RIVER ROVERS

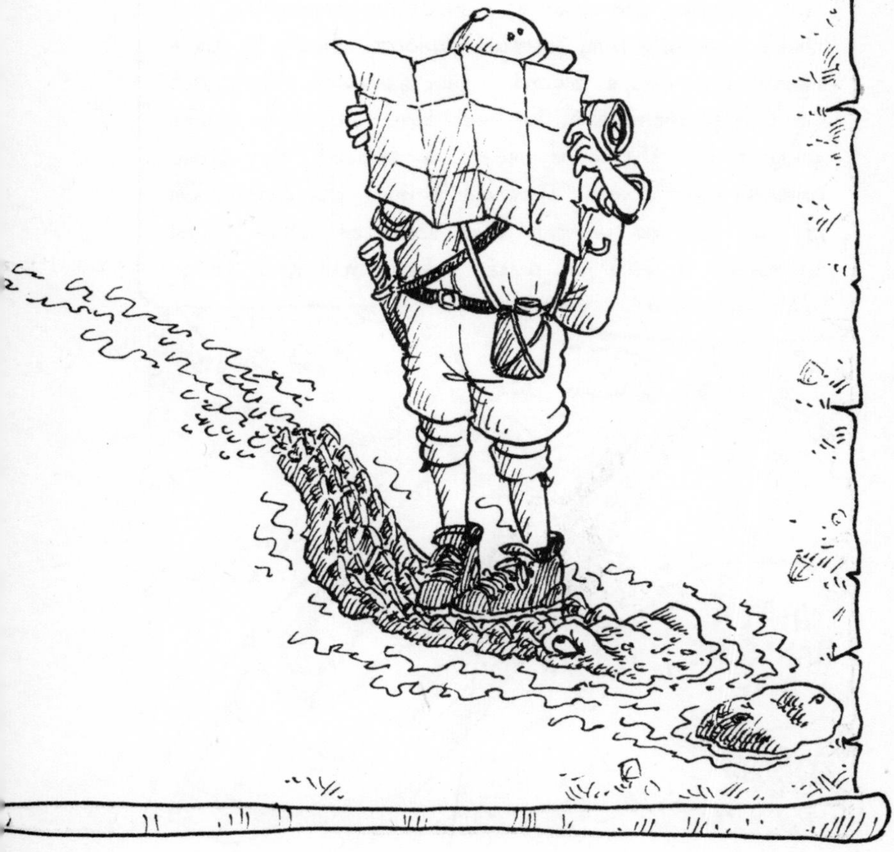

After a long, hard day at school, what could be better for getting rid of the stresses and strains than messing about on a river? Picture the scene. The birds are tweeting, the fish are jumping and the water's sparkling in the sunshine. Double geography seems a thing of the past. What could be more relaxing? But before you get too settled, remember – rivers aren't all sweetness and light. Some of them rush through the wildest parts of the world, and come complete with raging rapids, deadly river diseases and cranky, man-eating crocodiles. And that's precisely why intrepid explorers flock to their banks, like wasps around a jam sandwich. They just can't help themselves. So next time you think you're going round the bend, spare a thought for these restless river rovers. They didn't mind the danger. Oh no. So it's no wonder that some of them found themselves in very hot water indeed. Still keen to go with the flow?

Earth-shattering fact
When he found himself in deep trouble, roving Scottish explorer Joseph Thomson (1858–1895) had a barmy but brilliant trick up his sleeve. On one trip to explore the rivers of Africa, he was ambushed by unfriendly locals. But jokey Joseph didn't try to fight back. Instead he whipped out his two false front teeth. And that's the honest tooth, sorry, truth. His attackers were so gobsmacked they let him go and ran away.

WORST DENTAL WORK I'VE EVER SEEN!

Rambling Raleigh

Like joking Joseph Thomson, ace British sailor Walter Raleigh loved an adventure. Something he could get his teeth into. But in setting off to search for the legendary land of El Dorado in South America, you could say that rambling Raleigh bit off a lot more than he could chew.

Horrible Geography Travellers' Tales

SIR WALTER RALEIGH (1554–1618) NATIONALITY: ENGLISH

Remember the Spanish conquistadors (see page 104)? In the sixteenth century, they'd gone to South America and got filthy rich by killing the locals and stealing their gold. Well, Queen Elizabeth I of England was green with envy. Spain was England's arch enemy, and Liz desperately wanted to get her hands on some of that lovely loot. So she decided to send her trustiest sea captain, Sir Walter Raleigh, to grab a cut of the profits. Sensible Sir Walter leaped at the chance. (Actually, he had no choice. If he'd refused, the Queen would have chopped off his head, which would have been a real pain in the neck.)

In 1595, Sir Walter set off for South America. His mission was to find the fabled city of El Dorado, famous for its dazzling wealth. It was rumoured to lie deep in the rambling rainforest of Colombia. Raleigh had read all about it in a Spanish report which might have gone something like this...

Ye olde legende of El Dorado

The site of El Dorado was said to be Lake Guatavita near Bogotá. Legend said that in ancient times an unusual ceremony took place on the lake. Each year, a local king floated out on to the lake on a raft, with a great, glittering pile of gold and emeralds. The king himself was covered from head to toe in a shimmering powder made of real gold. That's how he got his name, El Dorado (in Spanish, this means the Golden Man). When he reached the middle of the lake, the king threw his priceless cargo into the water as an offering to the gods.

THIS IS COSTING ME A FORTUNE

> **Earth-shattering fact**
> Rumour had it that the bottom of the lake must be
> covered in a priceless carpet of gold and precious stones. A
> real sunken treasure trove. Hundreds of Spanish
> expeditions set out to seek their fortune. There was just
> one tiny problem – how on Earth could they get the gold
> out? In 1545, Jimenez de Quesada tried to drain the lake
> dry. Of course, he didn't do the work himself. That
> would have been much too draining. He organized a line
> of men with hollowed-out gourds (giant vegetables)
> instead of buckets. And it worked – sort of. De Quesada
> lowered the water level by three metres and salvaged
> thousands of gleaming gold coins.

Up the Orinoco

After a dreadful journey during which he lost two of his
ships, Raleigh landed in Trinidad. There he set fire to a
Spanish settlement and took the governor captive, just to
show him who was boss. Then he got ready for his treasure
hunt. The governor gave Raleigh a warning – the only
way through the rainforest was along the odious
Orinoco River. He'd have to face unfriendly locals and
wild animals and run the risk of getting hopelessly lost.
But that didn't put Raleigh off. With the governor and
some local guides to show him the way, he and his crew
set off to canoe up the river. It was gruelling going. They
were bitten alive by mosquitoes and kept losing their way
in the muddlesome maze of streams and creeks. Well, he
had been warned.

For three weeks they struggled on, but all they
found were a few measly gold mines. Then it started to
rain. But this wasn't a refreshing shower. This was a
devastating downpour and it certainly put a dampener
on things.

Within days, the sleepy Orinoco turned into a raging torrent. Raleigh remarked:

Our hearts were cold to behold the great rage and increase of the Orinoco.

Reluctantly, Raleigh was forced to turn back. His dreams of untold riches were a complete wash-out. Not only had he not found El Dorado – he didn't even come close.

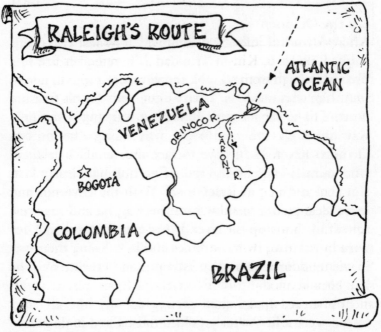

Weary Sir Walter returned to England, empty-handed. Needless to say, Queen Elizabeth was not amused.

South America again

From then on, things went from bad to worse for Sir Walter. In 1603 Queen Elizabeth died and the new king, James I, accused Walter of plotting against him and had him thrown into the Tower of London, where he spent the next 14 years.

... A FEW PICTURES, SOME CURTAINS, MY CHAIR IN THAT CORNER... YES, THIS WILL DO FINE.

Then, in 1616, King James had a change of heart. He released Raleigh from the Tower and ordered him to sail to South America again in a last-ditch attempt to find El Dorado. (The king hadn't suddenly turned into a softie. Actually, he was strapped for cash and needed Raleigh to find him some gold. But the political situation had changed and the crafty king didn't want any trouble with Spain.)

When he finally reached South America the following year, Raleigh fell sick and was too woefully weak to lead the expedition himself. So he sent his son, Wat, to find El Dorado instead, with strict orders not to upset the Spanish. Unfortunately, Wat didn't listen to a word his dad said. He and his companions attacked a Spanish settlement and Wat ended up being killed.

Once again Sir Walter returned to England in disgrace. As soon as he landed, he was arrested and thrown in the Tower. And this time, he finally lost his head. No, he really

161

did. To keep the peace with Spain, the king had to act … fast, and Walter's head was on the block. He was beheaded on 29 October 1618. Afterwards, his wife took her husband's head home in a leather bag. She kept it in a cupboard and showed it to visitors.

As for El Dorado, despite one expedition after another, it has never been found to this day.

Earth-shattering fact
In 1904, a British building firm made a daring attempt to find El Dorado. Their plan was to dig a series of tunnels and drain Lake Guatavita from underneath. They lowered the water level but were left with a sea of mud which dried rock-hard like concrete. By the time they'd fetched their drilling equipment, the lake had filled up again. In 1965, the government of Colombia banned any further exploration of the legendary lake.

South America was also the destination of one of the most famous river rovers ever. This posh French noble was incredibly brave and intrepid, and incredibly curious about what made the world tick. Believe it or not, his main reasons for going exploring weren't fame or fortune, but horrible science and geography. Are you ready to meet him?

Incredible La Condamine

This is the story of a man whose life was shaped by this earth-shattering question. Was the Earth shaped like a squashed tomato or was it more like a giant boiled egg?

Horrible Geography Travellers' Tales

CHARLES-MARIE
DE LA CONDAMINE
(1701 - 1774)
NATIONALITY:
FRENCH

Young Charles-Marie's family was frightfully posh and rich. When he was 18, he became a soldier and fought in a war. But his dream was to become a geodesist*.

*A gee-odd-esist's a scientist who studies the size and shape of the Earth.

As it turned out, Charles-Marie didn't have long to wait. In the 1730s a bitter row broke out at the Academy of Sciences in Paris about the Earth's exact shape. Wanna know what all the fuss was about? Here's two squabbling geographers to fill you in on the baffling details:

What on Earth are they talking about?

*Roughly translated, an oblate spheroid's a slightly squashed circle. And a prolate spheroid's a circle that's been stretched. Sort of. Confused? You're in good company. By the way, the reason horrible geographers needed to know the shape of the planet was to make navigation — that's finding the way from A to B — more accurate, and stop explorers getting horribly lost.

Before the whole thing went pear-shaped, the Academy decided to send out two expeditions to settle the matter – one to the Arctic and the other to South America. And guess who was chosen to lead the South American trip? Brilliant La Condamine, of course. He set sail from France in May 1735, with a boatload of bad-tempered geographers and all their Earth-measuring gear. They were still bickering as they set off. A year later, they rambled through bloomin' rainforests and reached the city of Quito, high up in the Andes Mountains in Peru (though it's now in Ecuador).

La Condamine's route

ATLANTIC OCEAN

CARTEGENA

VENEZUELA

QUITO

COLOMBIA

CUENCA

AMAZON R.

ECUADOR

BRAZIL

PERU

PACIFIC OCEAN

BOLIVIA

If postcards had been invented then, La Condamine might have sent one like this to his boss back home.

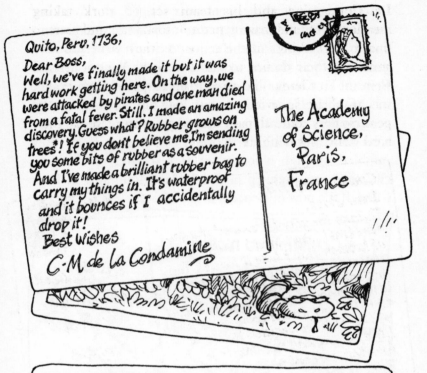

Quito, Peru, 1736,

Dear Boss,
Well, we've finally made it but it was hard work getting here. On the way, we were attacked by pirates and one man died from a fatal fever. Still, I made an amazing discovery. Guess what? Rubber grows on trees*! If you don't believe me, I'm sending you some bits of rubber as a souvenir. And I've made a brilliant rubber bag to carry my things in. It's waterproof and it bounces if I accidentally drop it!
Best Wishes
C·M de La Condamine

The Academy of Science, Paris, France

*La Condamine was right, of course. Rubber's made from the milky sap of rubber trees that grow in the South American rainforest. When news of his discovery reached Europe, it caused a massive stir and before long the rubber business was booming.

GIVE ME BACK MY RUBBER BONE

La Condamine and his team set to work taking measurements and making maps. It took years and years to finally work things out. But just as they were about to announce their findings, disaster struck. A letter arrived from the Academy. The other team had proved the Earth was an oblate spheroid, it said, and pipped them to the post. So they could all pack up and go home. After all their hard work, it was a bitter blow.

Cuenca, Peru, 1739,
Dear Boss,
Thanks for your letter and the good news (Pah! I don't think). I'm afraid some of the men didn't take it too well. Two went mad, one fell off a ladder and died, and one was murdered by an angry mob in the bullring (it had something to do with a girl, I'm told). I won't come home just yet, thanks. I've decided to take a little holiday and sail down the Amazon. See you soon.
Best wishes
C-M de La Condamine

The Academy
of Science,
Paris,
France

I AM HERE!

Amazon adventure

Some holiday it turned out to be. Curious La Condamine decided to take the long way home, along the awesome Amazon River and all the way to the Atlantic Ocean. But it wasn't plain sailing. His four-month journey took him deep into dense jungle and uncharted waters, where angry alligators and peckish piranha fish were known to lurk. For most of the way La Condamine travelled by canoe or flimsy raft. Once the raft got hopelessly caught up in a whirlpool, spinning round and round for hours on end. Besides, the weather was horribly hot and humid, and he was plagued by maddening swarms of mosquitoes and flies.

But for our hardy hero, it was heavenly. He was so busy noting down everything he'd seen, he only had time to scribble one last postcard home.

The Amazon River, 1743

Dear Boss,
What a place! I'm having an amazing time. I've made loads of notes about the river and its wonderful wildlife. The jungle on the riverbank's stuffed full of bloomin' plants and animals. But did you know there aren't any poisonous snakes in the whole of the Amazon*? Amazing, isn't it? I think I might get a nice little snake for a pet. Must dash. Lots to do. C-M de La Condamine

The Academy of Science, Paris, France

*Horrible Health Warning
Oops. If you're out and about in the Amazon rainforest, don't listen to La Condamine's crackpot tip. Some deadly poisonous snakes do lurk in the bloomin' rainforest. So La Condamine was wrong. Dead wrong. Even a jaguar would be a much safer bet as a pet. Compared to some of these revolting reptiles, it's a pussycat.

Incredible La Condamine reached home in 1745 and was given a hero's welcome. It was the first time a river had been explored simply for science's sake. For curious La Condamine was more of a nature rambler than a river rover. His notebook was crammed full of notes, maps and sketches about the river and the people and wildlife he'd seen, and that other horrible geographers had never seen before.

Earth-shattering fact
Explorers often face danger — it goes with the territory. Take posh German geographer Baron Alexander von Humboldt (1769–1859). In 1799 Alexander set off for South America. And he suffered horribly;
• *On his journey down the Orinoco River he was badly bitten by mosquitoes.*
• *His food ran out and he had to live on ants and dried cocoa beans, washed down by rancid river water.*

I HATE HAVING ANTS FOR TEA!

- *He (deliberately) drank some deadly poison to see if it would make him ill. (It did, but not fatally.)*
- *And then he gave himself a nasty shock by picking up an electric eel. Bet you wouldn't suffer like that for geography?*

Elsewhere in the world, river roving was positively surging ahead. Now horrible geographers set their sights on the awesome rivers of Africa. And they needed a willing victim, sorry, volunteer. By chance, a famous intrepid explorer had a bit of free time on his hands…

Long-lost Livingstone

It wasn't easy being a superstar explorer and a legend in your own lifetime. You couldn't go anywhere without people wanting to know your every move. So imagine the massive stir it caused when legendary David Livingstone went and got hopelessly lost.

Horrible Geography Travellers' Tales

Life was tough for young David. His family was so poor that he never went to school and at the age of ten he had to go to work in a factory. But in his spare time David always had his nose in a book and taught himself science and geography.

He was obviously a brilliant teacher and student because later he went to university and trained as a doctor. He was also very religious. When he'd finished his studies, he went off to Africa to work as a missionary*.

*A missionary's someone who travels and spreads their religious ideas. David thought if he taught others about his Christian faith, he'd help them to live better lives. Did it work? Well, some people didn't like David's meddling. But others listened to what he said because, well, he was such a jolly nice chap.

But Livingstone was soon bitten by the exploring bug and there was no turning back. For 30 years he criss-crossed the continent, travelling to places where no outsiders had ever set foot before. He discovered lakes and rivers, including the mighty Zambezi, which no Europeans knew existed (though, of course, the locals had always known they were there).

In the course of his travels, intrepid Livingstone covered thousands of kilometres, mostly by foot. He suffered terribly from deadly tropical diseases and was once badly mauled by a lion. But even that didn't put him off. In 1865, after a trip back home to Britain, he set off for Africa again on another great adventure. This time he wanted to search for the source (that's the place where the river begins) of the raging River Nile.

Livingstone gets lost

Now you might think tracking down the source of a river was simple. As simple as finding out where your mum's hidden your favourite comic until you've finished your geography homework. Especially when the river in question is the longest in the world. Easy peasy. But you'd be wrong. Horribly wrong. For hundreds of years, the source of the Nile remained one of geography's best-kept secrets. Usually the source is a mountain stream, or a glacier, or even a lake. But top geographers didn't have a clue where on Earth the Nile began. Several expeditions set off to get to the bottom of things but they all ended in failure. Now it was Livingstone's turn to take up the search. After all, he was Britain's greatest living explorer so it should have been a walk in the park. Things started off swimmingly…

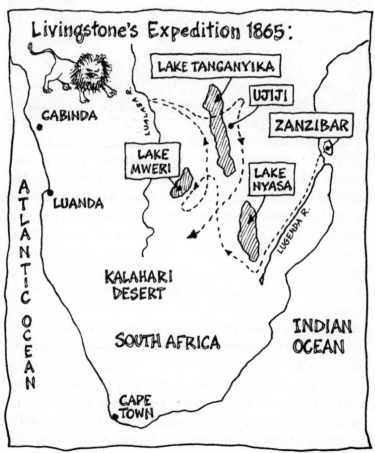

In August 1865 Livingstone set sail from England for Africa. When he reached the River Lualaba, Livingstone was sure he'd found the source of the Nile at last. But before he could prove it, things took a terrible turn. Half of his companions fell sick, died or ran away. Livingstone himself was seriously ill and, to make matters worse, someone pinched his medicine chest.

Half-dead and a bag of bones, he managed to struggle to Ujiji, a village on the edge of Lake Tanganyika. Out of sight and out of mind.

Back home, nothing was heard of Livingstone for years and years. In fact he was given up for lost. He was still Britain's most famous explorer. *Dead* famous, everyone thought.

Stanley saves the day

In America, though, people still believed Livingstone might be alive. And the *New York Herald* newspaper sent a roving reporter to find him and bring him back. The reporter's name was Henry Morton Stanley (1841–1904).

Stanley's childhood had been even unhappier than Livingstone's. If you think you've got it tough having to tidy your room and do the washing-up, get a load of this. Young Henry was abandoned by his parents and sent to live in a wretched workhouse. Then he ran away to sea. He ended up in America where, after working as a soldier and sailor, he got a job as a journalist. Now he was off to Africa to look for long-lost Livingstone. Did he find the intrepid explorer? Or was he woefully off course? Stanley sent his roving reports back home to his newspaper. Luckily the *Daily Globe* managed to grab a copy of his sensational scoop.

11 NOV · *The Daily Globe* · 1871

UJIJI, EAST AFRICA
HOW I FOUND LIVINGSTONE
by Henry Morton Stanley

It was a historic moment. Yesterday, in Ujiji, I met Dr David Livingstone. I couldn't believe my luck. Britain's greatest living explorer has been missing for years but after months of searching, I had found him at last.

My search for Dr Livingstone began way back in March. I decided to retrace the last known route he had taken. It was a hard slog in the sweltering heat, and many of my men were struck down by disease. I myself fell ill with a

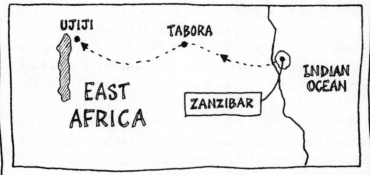

fever and was on the point of turning back when news reached me that a sick old white man had been seen in Ujiji, only a few days' march away. My heart missed a beat. It must be Livingstone, I thought, and we grimly plodded on.

To my amazement, it was. When I finally came face to face with my hero, I admit I was lost for words. But I was shocked at his appearance. He looked terribly thin and weary, with a grey beard and moustache. Still, I was so pleased to see him I wanted to shout and cheer. Somehow I held myself in check and instead I walked up to him, doffed my hat and said, "Dr Livingstone, I presume?" With a kind smile, he replied, "Yes."

It seems that my arrival came just in the nick of time. The doctor was sick and frail, and in dire need of food and medicines. I was only too pleased to help. I also brought him news from home which really cheered him up. What an astonishing man he is. Kind-hearted and gentle, he never complains about a thing, despite all the hardships he's been through. We hit it off immediately and became the best of friends.

STANLEY MEETS LIVINGSTONE

Back to the source

The two men spent several months together exploring some nearby rivers. Then Stanley made a quick trip to London but Livingstone refused to go with him. In 1872 he set off up the River Lualaba to continue his search for the source of the Nile. Sadly, it was to be Livingstone's last intrepid trip. Worn out by all the travelling, he died on 1 May 1873. His faithful servant buried his heart in Africa, according to his dying wish.

After his pal Livingstone's death, Stanley returned to Africa and took up the search for the source of the Nile again. To cut a long story short, in 1874 he finally solved the mystery, once and for all. So had legendary Livingstone been right all along?

Earth-shattering fact
I'm afraid not. The source of the River Nile turned out to be a river which flowed out of Lake Victoria over a waterfall called Ripon Falls. And, annoyingly, it had already been discovered by British explorer John Hanning Speke (1827–1864) 12 years earlier. Stanley simply proved it was true. As for the River Lualaba? Well, it had nothing to do with the Nile. Yes, it flowed into a river – but it was the mighty River Congo.

I THOUGHT I WAS FOLLOWING A RIVER, BUT IT'S A CREASE IN THE MAP!

So Stanley went on to become a famous explorer in his own right (though some people said he was far too big for his boots). He was the first outsider to follow the River Congo (now also called the River Zaire) all the way to sea, though in doing so he almost ended up in a cannibal's cooking pot. And he wasn't the only explorer who narrowly escaped that grisly fate...

Amazing Mary

This story is about an amazing woman. At a time when respectable girls were expected to stay at home and look after the house, Mary set off for Africa to bone up on fish.

Horrible Geography Travellers' Tales

Mary Kingsley didn't have time to go to school. She was too busy at home, looking after her poorly mum and her sickly little brother. You see, her dad was away a lot. Then, when Mary was 30, her mum and dad both died. Suddenly Mary was free to do whatever she wanted to. (By this time, her brother had buzzed off on his own travels.) Her friends made some helpful suggestions. What about a sightseeing trip to Europe? That was the ladylike thing to do. Or perhaps a nice holiday by the sea? But daring Mary had other ideas. She decided to set off for Africa to do a spot of exploring. (Her friends were horrified.)

Mary's awesome African adventures

In 1893, Mary spent a year in Africa. But that was just the start of it. Mary had such itchy feet that the following year she was off on her intrepid travels again. And this time her brilliant excuse was ... fish. Yep, fish. The British Museum in London asked Mary to collect specimens of some rare African fish. Trouble is, the rivers these rare fish lived in were horribly risky to reach. Why? Well, some seriously unfriendly cannibals lived in the rainforests along their banks. And, frighteningly, these cannibals were called the Fang. Was Mary worried? Quite the opposite. She couldn't wait to be off and in December 1894 she set sail for Africa again.

A year later, Mary was back in England. And we sent our *Daily Globe* reporter along to find out more about her trail-blazing trip.

Where have you just come back from?

I've been in West Africa, exploring the Ogowe and Rembwe rivers and searching for rare fish. Are you fond of fish, dear? They're fascinating creatures, I think.

Er, right. So how did you get about?

For the first stretch of the journey, I went by paddle steamer. Very comfortable. But it couldn't go over the rapids so I had to carry on by canoe. It was all right apart from the capsizing. Oh, and a spot of bother with some crocodiles. I bashed one on the nose with a paddle. That showed it who was boss.

I bet. What was the strangest place you stayed in?

It was a Fang village called Efoua. People thought I was mad to go there. The Fang are cannibals, you see, and I could easily have ended up in the pot. But I gave them some cloth and fish hooks and they were very friendly to me. Perhaps they just weren't hungry. Chicken drumstick, dear?

Fang-tastic, I mean fantastic. And what was your worst moment?

Hmm, let me see. One day I noticed a very strong pong coming from a bag in my hut. It was a horrid sickly sort of smell like gone-off fish. (A smell I know very well.) What a whiff. I emptied the bag into my hat and you'll never guess what was in it – a human hand and a selection of toes, eyes and ears (all quite fresh)! Are you all right, dear? You've gone rather green. It turned out that the Fang like to keep a bit of everyone they eat as a souvenir. Fascinating, isn't it?

Gulp! What essentials do you always pack?

For travelling, I like to wear a white blouse and a long black skirt with big pockets for my penknife, notebook, compass and, of course, a nice clean hanky.

I pop on a pair of my brother's old trousers under my skirt — they're brilliant for keeping off leeches when I'm squelching through swamps. Oh, and I always pack a small revolver (though I've never used it yet). And some nets and bottles for catching all those lovely fish

But doesn't a long skirt get in the way?

Oh no, dear. Quite the opposite, in fact. My skirt once saved my life. You see, I fell down a pit in the jungle (it was used for catching animals), lined with nasty sharp spikes. Luckily, my skirt cushioned my fall and stopped me getting badly stabbed. If I'd been wearing trousers, I'd have been a goner. So I can thank my lucky skirt that I'm still alive.

What do you do when you're not travelling?

I'm going to write a book about my travels in west Africa. I thought I'd call it 'Travels in West Africa' – it's a catchy title, don't you think? I also give lectures and talks to learned geographical societies. That's much more nerve-racking, I can tell you, than staying the night with a Fang family.

Did you bring back any souvenirs of your trip?

Not souvenirs exactly. But I collected 65 brand new types of fish. Actually, three of them have been named after me, so I'm awfully chuffed. Oh, and I brought back quite a few beetles – bigger than anything we get here. Would you like to see them, dear? They're real beauties.

Er, no, thanks, I'll give it a miss. So where are you off to next?

Oh, back to west Africa, I hope. The sooner, the better. There are plenty more fish in the sea, well, river, for me to catch. Now, dear, how about another nice cup of tea?

But Mary wasn't the only woman to take the plunge and make her name as an intrepid explorer. Many other daring women were willing to leave their boring home lives behind and go with the flow.

More women river rovers

Isabela Godin (1729–1792) was married to French explorer, Jean Godin. In 1749, Jean and Isabela decided to go home to France. So Jean set off down the Amazon River to check out their rambling route. But he didn't come back. Fed up with waiting, Isabela set out to find him. It was a dreadful journey. One by one, her companions dropped like flies until only Isabela was left. She stumbled on alone, starving and nearly dead. Amazingly, she made it to the coast alive, and she and Jean were finally reunited … after 20 years apart!

Alexandrine Tinné (1835–1869) was brave and slightly batty – a great combination for an explorer. In 1861, she set off in a boat to explore the River Nile, accompanied by her mum and her auntie. She also took along 500 local guides, a load of donkeys and 65 soldiers for good measure. Sadly, her mum and auntie died but Alexandrine was hooked on Africa. In 1869, she tried to become the first woman to cross the Sahara Desert but was murdered by unfriendly locals.

Florence Baker (1841–1916) was the wife of British explorer, Samuel Baker. The story goes that he spotted her in a slave-market in Hungary and fell in love with her at first sight. From then on, they were never apart. In 1861, they went off together to Africa to search for the source of the Nile. It was  gruelling. But despite the heat, the flies and the danger, Florence never complained. Even when dinner was tough hippo steak, washed down with champagne. (They didn't find the Nile's source, of course, but they did discover Lake Albert and the massive Kabalega Falls which no Europeans had ever seen before.)

You've climbed the highest mountains, sailed the world's stormiest seas, braved bone-chilling temperatures and ridden the river rapids with some of the greatest explorers in the world. And, as you've found out, it hasn't all been easy. So here's the BIG QUESTION. Why on Earth are some people *still* willing to face horrible hardships, homesickness and even death to blaze new and far-flung trails? Why not ask them for yourself? The next chapter's all about intrepid modern explorers. You might just catch them before they wander off.

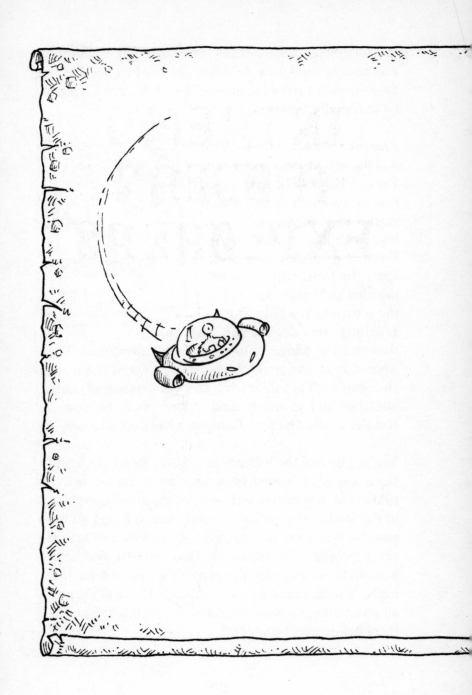

INTREPID MØDERN EXPLØRERS

Explorers today are still amazingly bold and adventurous, but they are just as interested in geography and science as derring-do. Now they also want to find out what makes the world tick. All over the world, wild places and the people who live there are being destroyed as horrible humans need more land to live in and more natural resources, such as oil and timber. The job of many modern explorers is to find ways of protecting the planet, its people and wildlife for the future, before it's too late.

And there are still plenty of people who are prepared to push the boat out in the quest for adventure. Thanks to these intrepid modern explorers we now know what lurks in the depths of the odious oceans and at the tops of the freakiest peaks. And most of the remaining gaps in the maps have now been filled in.

Unlike explorers long ago, intrepid modern explorers have lots of mod cons to help them, such as mobile phones to keep in touch and satellites for navigation. Which is lucky. But exploring the world's wild places is still a horribly risky thing to do. Think you've got what it takes? Check out the amazing feats of these modern-day explorers. We caught up with them at the annual Golden Globe Intrepid Explorers' Awards.

Intrepid Explorer Awards

The *Daily Globe* asked readers to vote for their top modern-day explorers. And picking the winner has been a very close-run thing. Here's Miles to announce the results.

Longest journey
Runner-up

In 1968, British explorer Wally Herbert (born 1934) set off on a perilous trip. With three companions and their dog teams, he left Alaska and travelled a staggering 5,820 kilometres right across the Arctic Ocean to Spitzbergen in Norway, via the perishing North Pole. It was the longest sledge journey ever and took a gruelling 476 days. And it was no polar picnic. They were pestered by peckish polar bears and every day the pack ice threatened to break up and send them plummeting into the freezing cold sea.

And the winner is...

Between 1979 and 1982 British explorer Ranulph Fiennes (born 1944) led an extraordinary expedition from the Antarctic to the Arctic, stopping off at the South and North Poles. From Pole to Pole, that's a distance of over 12,000 kilometres. An awesome achievement. Daring Ranulph's also explored the River Nile and found a lost desert city in Arabia. And after one trip to the perishing Poles, he had to cut off his own frostbitten fingers. The things he missed most on his trips? A nice long soak in a hot bath and chocolate. Congratulations, Ranulph. A worthy winner.

Luckiest to be alive
Runner-up

American Eric Hansen (born 1948) has diced with death all over the world and was once shipwrecked on a desert island. In the 1980s, plucky Eric spent months in the rainforests of Borneo, armed with only a bed sheet, a change of clothes and some goods to trade. Most of the places he visited were marked "unknown" on the map. He travelled almost 4,000 kilometres by foot and dug-out canoe. His problems started when the locals mistook him for an evil spirit who killed people and sucked their blood. Not surprisingly, Eric was outta there like a shot.

And the winner is...

In 1947, Norwegian Thor Heyerdahl (1914-2002) set sail on an epic voyage. He sailed 7,000 kilometres from Callao in Peru to the Tuamoto Islands in the South Pacific ... on a flimsy balsa-wood raft called Kon-Tiki. Intrepid Thor wanted to prove that the islands' first settlers came from South America and not from Asia as the experts thought. For 101 days, Thor and his crew drifted through violent storms and shark-infested waters before they finally washed ashore on a coral reef. A brilliant achievement for someone who was SCARED STIFF of water.

Most intrepid explorer
Runner-up

In the 1940s, British explorer Wilfred Thesiger (born 1910) crossed the Empty Quarter in the Arabian Desert not once but twice on camel-back. This desperate desert's not called empty for nothing. There's nothing to see for miles and miles except scorching seas of sand dunes. Thesiger nearly died of thirst and had to go days without food. He also spent five years living with the local people and learning desert lore. His top tip for budding explorers? Never drink water your camel has peed in. Excellent advice.

And the winner is...

Italian Reinhold Messner (born 1944) is probably the greatest modern-day mountaineer. Between 1970 and 1986, Reinhold became the first person to climb all 14 of the world's highest peaks (those more than 8,000 metres tall). To top it all, he was also the first person to climb Mount Everest without oxygen and the first to climb it solo (without ropes or guides). And he's walked to the South Pole. So well done, Reinhold. An outstanding performance.

Earth-shattering fact

If there was a prize for taking the plunge, there'd be no doubt about the winners. On 23 January 1960, Dr Jacques Piccard and Lieutenant Don Walsh of the US Navy dived almost 11 kilometres to the bottom of the Marianas Trench in the Pacific Ocean – the DEEPEST PLACE ON THE PLANET. They made their death-defying descent in a bathyscaphe (BATH-ee-scafe), a sort of mini sub, called Trieste. It took a nail-biting four hours and 48 minutes to reach the bottom. At any moment Trieste might have cracked under the pressure of all the water weighing down on it.

OFF TO THE BOTTOM OF THE ODIOUS OCEAN

But it was worth all the worry. When they switched on the floodlights, they saw a world no one had ever seen before – the deepest, darkest depths of the ocean. And a ghostly white flat fish staring back at them. Their treacherous trip took eight and a half hours – a record-breaking dive that still stands today. And one of the greatest feats of ocean exploration ever.

An intrepid new life

Still want to become an explorer? Well, even though it's so quick and easy to get about by plane, train and car and the world is becoming a very small place, there are still plenty of wild things to see and do.

Perhaps you fancy having a go at the explorers' grand slam? You have to climb the world's seven highest peaks and reach the North and South Poles. How intrepid is that? And only four people have ever done it.

Or you could head for the jungle. You might find a rainforest bloomer that doctors could use to save people's lives. About a quarter of modern medicines come from rainforest plants.

While you're trying to decide, just remember one thing. Being an explorer can be horrible. Horribly tiring and uncomfortable and even downright dangerous. But it can also be horribly exciting and fascinating too. You never know what's around the corner, especially if you haven't got a map. And that's the earth-shattering truth!

INTREPID EXPLORERS TIMELINE

ANCIENT TIMES

1500 BC   1250 BC   1000 BC   750 BC   500 BC

a) c. 1492 BC Queen Hatshepsut (Egypt)

c. 1000 BC The Polynesians start exploring the Pacific Ocean

c. 600 BC Pharaoh Necho's Phoenician fleet sails around Africa

b) 470 BC Hanno the Phoenician (Carthage)

c) Fourth century BC Pytheas (Greece)

a) Destination: Punt
Sent a fleet of five ships and 250 sailors on a
sensational shopping spree down the coast of
Africa to the land of Punt.

I HOPE IT'S NOT HALF-DAY CLOSING!

194

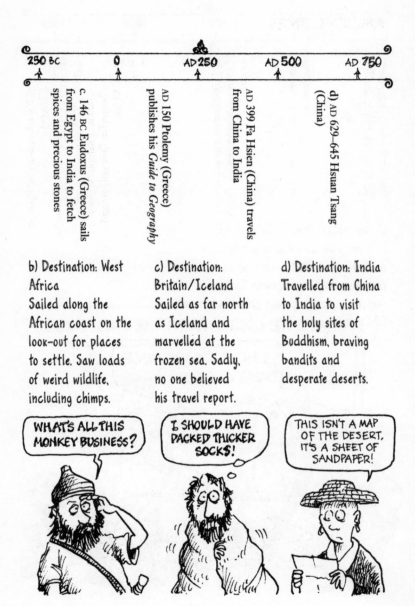

250 BC — 0 — AD 250 — AD 500 — AD 750

c. 146 BC Eudoxus (Greece) sails from Egypt to India to fetch spices and precious stones

AD 150 Ptolemy (Greece) publishes his *Guide to Geography*

AD 399 Fa Hsien (China) travels from China to India

d) AD 629–645 Hsuan Tsang (China)

b) Destination: West Africa
Sailed along the African coast on the look-out for places to settle. Saw loads of weird wildlife, including chimps.

WHAT'S ALL THIS MONKEY BUSINESS?

c) Destination: Britain/Iceland
Sailed as far north as Iceland and marvelled at the frozen sea. Sadly, no one believed his travel report.

I SHOULD HAVE PACKED THICKER SOCKS!

d) Destination: India
Travelled from China to India to visit the holy sites of Buddhism, braving bandits and desperate deserts.

THIS ISN'T A MAP OF THE DESERT, IT'S A SHEET OF SANDPAPER!

195

THE MIDDLE AGES

900 — 950 — 1000 — 1050 — 1100

c. AD 860 St Brendan (Ireland)
possibly sails to North America

a) Tenth century AD The Vikings
(Scandinavia)

c. AD 1000 Leif Ericsson
(Norway) sails to Vinland
Canada)

AD 1095 The Crusader Knights
travel from Europe to Jerusalem

a) Destination: Greenland/Iceland
Left home because things got horribly
crowded. Pretended Greenland was green
and grassy to get people to live there.

PERHAPS WE COULD **PAINT** THE SNOW GREEN?

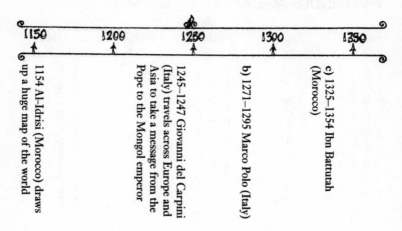

1150 | 1200 | 1250 | 1300 | 1350

1154 Al-Idrisi (Morocco) draws up a huge map of the world

1245–1247 Giovanni del Carpini (Italy) travels across Europe and Asia to take a message from the Pope to the Mongol emperor

b) 1271–1295 Marco Polo (Italy)

c) 1325–1354 Ibn Battutah (Morocco)

b) Destination: China
Travelled to China along the old Silk Road. Spent the next 17 years working as a roving ambassador for Kublai Khan.

c) Destination: Middle East / Sahara Desert
Spent 30 years on the road, visiting the holy sites of Islam. Covered over 120,000 kilometres by foot, camel, ship and canoe.

197

FIFTEENTH & SIXTEENTH CENTURIES

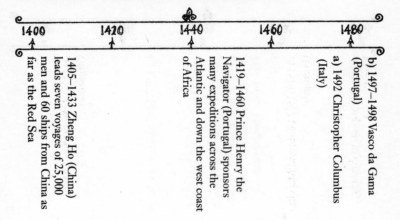

1400   1420   1440   1460   1480

1405–1433 Zheng Ho (China) leads seven voyages of 25,000 men and 60 ships from China as far as the Red Sea

1419–1460 Prince Henry the Navigator (Portugal) sponsors many expeditions across the Atlantic and down the west coast of Africa

a) 1492 Christopher Columbus (Italy)

b) 1497–1498 Vasco da Gama (Portugal)

a) Destination: North/South America
The first European to find the Americas (though the Vikings might have got there before him). He thought he'd reached Asia.

b) Destination: India
The first European to sail to India. Opened up a brand-new sea route from Europe to Asia.

1500	1520	1540	1560	1580

1513 Ponce de Leon (Spain) is the first European to discover Florida, USA

c) 1519–1522 Ferdinand Magellan (Portugal)

1540–1542 Francisco de Orellana (Spain) becomes the first European to travel down the River Amazon to the sea

d) 1577–1580 Francis Drake (England)

c) Destination: Around the world Led the first expedition to sail around the world but was killed in a fight and didn't make it back home.

d) Destination: Around the world Led the second expedition to sail around the world. On the way, plundered Spanish treasure ships and made a fortune

THIS TRIP IS COSTING A FORTUNE...

THIS TRIP IS MAKING A FORTUNE...

SEVENTEENTH & EIGHTEENTH CENTURIES

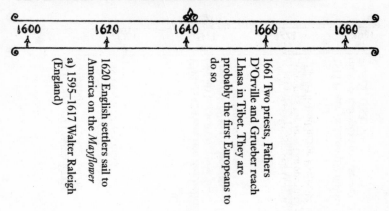

1600   1620   1640   1660   1680

a) 1595–1617 Walter Raleigh (England)

1620 English settlers sail to America on the *Mayflower*

1661 Two priests, Fathers D'Orville and Grueber reach Lhasa in Tibet. They are probably the first Europeans to do so

a) Destination: South America
Tried to find the legendary city of El Dorado, famous for its gold, but returned empty-handed and had his head chopped off instead.

b) Destination: River Amazon
Set off for South America to measure the shape of the Earth. Sailed down the Amazon River, dodging peckish piranha fish.

I THINK I'LL HAVE A LITTLE TAKEN OFF THE TOP, WHEN I GET BACK TO ENGLAND.

1700   1720   1740   1760   1780

1721 Jacob Roggeveen (Holland) becomes the first European to see Easter Island in the Pacific Ocean

b) 1735-1745 Charles-Marie de La Condamine (France)

c) 1766 Louis-Antoine de Bougainville (France)

d) 1768-1771; 1772-1775; 1776-1779 James Cook (Britain)

e) 1799 Alexander von Humboldt (Germany)

c) Destination: South Pacific
Led the first scientific expedition to sail around the world. Collected hundreds of plant and animal specimens, never seen in Europe before.

d) Destination: South Pacific/Southern Ocean
Led three daring voyages to the South Pacific and Southern Ocean. The first person to cross the Antarctic Circle and to sail around Antarctica but reckoned Antarctica didn't exist.

e) Destination: South America
Spent years travelling in South America, carrying out dicey nature experiments like picking up an electric eel and drinking deadly poison.

HMM, NOT BAD...

IT'S NOT THERE!

NINETEENTH CENTURY

1800 — 1805 — 1810 — 1815 — 1820

1804-1806 Lewis and Clark (USA) follow the Missouri River across America to the Pacific Ocean

1806 Mungo Park (Britain) leads an expedition to the River Niger in Africa

a) 1809–1811 Thomas Manning (Britain)

b) 1815 Johann Burckhardt (Switzerland)

1823 James Weddell (Britain) crosses the Antarctic Circle and explores the Weddell Sea

a) Destination: Lhasa, Tibet
One of the first Europeans to visit the closed city of Lhasa in Tibet, even though he really hated travelling.

b) Destination: Petra, Jordan
Rediscovered the long-lost desert city of Petra in Jordan. Was actually on his way to explore the River Niger at the time.

202

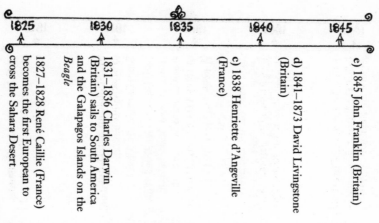

1825 1830 1835 1840 1845

1827–1828 René Caillié (France) becomes the first European to cross the Sahara Desert

1831–1836 Charles Darwin (Britain) sails to South America and the Galapagos Islands on the *Beagle*

c) 1838 Henriette d'Angeville (France)

d) 1841–1873 David Livingstone (Britain)

e) 1845 John Franklin (Britain)

c) Destination: Mont Blanc
The first woman to climb Mont Blanc, the highest peak in Europe. Even though climbing wasn't a very ladylike thing to do at the time.

d) Destination: Africa
Spent years exploring Africa and discovering new rivers and lakes. Went missing on his search for the source of the River Nile and was famously found by Stanley.

e) Destination: North-West Passage
Set off to search for a new trade route across the frozen north but was never seen again.

AM I LOST?

I DID GET LOST

203

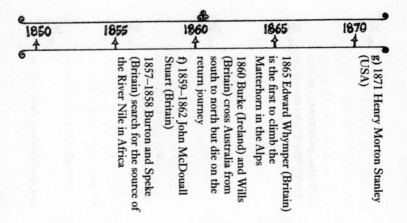

1850 · 1855 · 1860 · 1865 · 1870

the River Nile in Africa
(Britain) search for the source of
1857–1858 Burton and Speke

Stuart (Britain)
f) 1859–1862 John McDouall

return journey
south to north but die on the
(Britain) cross Australia from
1860 Burke (Ireland) and Wills

Matterhorn in the Alps
is the first to climb the
1865 Edward Whymper (Britain)

(USA)
g) 1871 Henry Morton Stanley

f) Destination: Australia
Led three expeditions to try to cross Australia from Adelaide to Darwin. It was third time lucky but his health suffered horribly.

g) Destination: Africa
Sent to Africa as a newspaper reporter to find long-lost Livingstone. Became the first outsider to sail up the River Congo (Zaire).

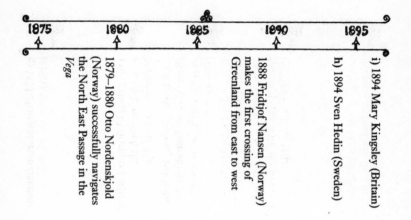

| 1875 | 1880 | 1885 | 1890 | 1895 |

1879–1880 Otto Nordenskjold (Norway) successfully navigates the North East Passage in the *Vega*

1888 Fridtjof Nansen (Norway) makes the first crossing of Greenland from east to west

h) 1894 Sven Hedin (Sweden)

i) 1894 Mary Kingsley (Britain)

h) Destination: Takla Makan Desert
Crossed the treacherous Takla Makan Desert, despite being warned off by the locals who called it the "Sea of Death".

i) Destination: Africa
Spent several years in Africa, searching for rare river fish. Stayed in a cannibal village and found a bag of body bits in her hut.

TWENTIETH CENTURY

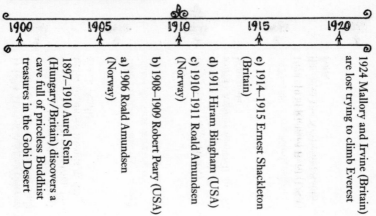

1897–1910 Aurel Stein (Hungary/Britain) discovers a cave full of priceless Buddhist treasures in the Gobi Desert

a) 1906 Roald Amundsen (Norway)

b) 1908–1909 Robert Peary (USA)

c) 1910–1911 Roald Amundsen (Norway)

d) 1911 Hiram Bingham (USA)

e) 1914–1915 Ernest Shackleton (Britain)

1924 Mallory and Irvine (Britain) are lost trying to climb Everest

a) Destination: North-West Passage
The first person to sail through the North-West Passage in his nippy boat, the Gjoa.

b) Destination: North Pole
The first person to reach the North Pole, even though rival explorer Frederick Cook claimed to have beaten him to it.

c) Destination: South Pole
The first person to reach the South Pole ... and to come back alive. A brilliantly planned expedition.

1925　1930　1935　1940　1945

1928–1930 Richard Byrd (USA) flies over the North and South Poles

1935 Jimmy Angel (USA) discovers the Angel Falls, the world's highest waterfall, in Venezuela

1947 Thor Heyerdahl (Norway) sails his Kon-Tiki raft from Peru to the Tuamoto Islands in the South Pacific

f) 1953 Tenzing Norgay (Nepal) Edmund Hillary (New Zealand)

d) Destination: Machu Picchu, Peru
Discovered the Inca city of Machu Picchu in Peru which had been lost for centuries.

e) Destination: Antarctica
Attempted to cross Antarctica but his ship got stuck in the ice. He and his men survived their appalling ordeal against all the odds.

f) Destination: Mount Everest
The first people to climb Mount Everest, on the border of Nepal and Tibet, the highest peak in the world.

LOST & FOUND

I THINK I'LL EXPLORE SOMEWHERE HOT NEXT TIME.

TOP OF THE WORLD!

If you're interested in finding out more about becoming an intrepid explorer, here are some websites you can visit:

www.rgs.org
The Royal Geographical Society's website. Click on the Expedition Advisory Centre to find out how to plan your own intrepid trip.

www.explorers.org
The website of the prestigous Explorers' Club in New York, USA. Information and news about the latest expeditions.

www.stanfords.co.uk
A brilliant shop selling map and travel guides so you don't get hopelessly lost.

www.bses.org.uk
The British Schools Exploring Society's website. The society offers opportunities for young people to take part in expeditions around the world.

www.theyet.org
The website of the Young Explorer's Trust. It gives training, support and advice to schools and young people trying to plan an expedition.